GREAT INNS *of* AMERICA ®

1988 - 1989 EDITION

THE KNAPP PRESS
LOS ANGELES

ISBN 0-89535-212-5 (pbk.)
Library of Congress Catalog Card No. 88-81441

FORWARD

Bringing special people and special places together is what Great Inns of America is all about. The inns in this guidebook are all members of Great Inns of America, a network of the best inns and innkeepers across the Nation. Of the thousands of inns in North America, we consider few to be in the class deserving the appellation "Great Inn".

These inns have evolved in various ways. Some are stately, some are informal, some have been around a long time, and some only seem that way. But all these inns share the same high quality standards and a brand of old fashioned hospitality and friendliness that immediately distinguish them as Great Inns of America.

To become a Great Inn, the inn must have on premises or adjacent fine dining, private bathrooms, and the array of services and facilities you expect to find in full service lodgings. In this guidebook you will find color pictures of each inn, maps, directions, a complete description of each inn, and the services and amenities available.

Great Inns are special places. Places where you can sleep in a yard deep feather bed and waken to smells of homemade bread. Places where your host can tell you the history of every piece of furniture in the house, the birth dates of the surrounding trees and the names of practically every guest entertained during the last 20 years.

These places still exist, in little towns, in rejuvenated sections of big cities, in the country, in the mountains and on the shore. They are special places for special people. It is this unique combination of setting, decor and personal touch that now offers a better travel experience to the discerning public.

Finding the right country inn or historic hotel has often been a difficult chore. We have made it easier with this guidebook and our toll free information and reservation number. Helping you find the Great Inn that is right for you is our goal.

If you are planning a trip, please give us a call. Allow us to help you locate an inn and send you their brochure. When you are ready to make your reservation we hope you will call us back so we can personally introduce you to the inn and the innkeeper. If you prefer, please feel free to call the inn directly.

We are confident that your stay will be enjoyable and we hope that you will become one of the increasing number of inn lovers throughout the United States and Canada.

Bill Gilbert
President, Great Inns of America

INDEX

PICKWICK HOTEL

1023 20th Street South, Birmingham, Alabama 35205
(205) 933-9555 (800) 255-7304

The Pickwick Hotel is located in the center of Birmingham's Five Points South Historic District, the city's premier restaurant and entertainment area. The neighborhood is like a village with a central plaza complete with fountain and numerous park benches. This popular area is enjoyed by both visitors and locals for its historic ambience, unique shops, and multitude of restaurants and lounges.

The Pickwick was built in 1931 as the Medical Arts Building, one of the Southeast's first medical office buildings, and it is on the National Register of Historic Places. The art deco style lobby and exterior remain the same, with the rest of the hotel completely renovated and showcasing the elegant features of the art deco design style.

Of special interest in the lobby area are the glass carvings, original artwork, marble entryway, sculptures, and antique bureaus. Behind the bar is a towering glass etching titled "The Pickwick Tango". These features give the hotel a cozy cosmopolitan atmosphere.

Adjoining the hotel is Pickwick Place, a shopping, dining, entertainment, and office plaza that cuts through the block. Pickwick Place establishments are varied and include an Italian Restaurant, specialty gift shop and a popular piano bar. One block from the hotel is Magnolia Park, a small scenic park popular for picnic lunches. Just beyond the park is an area containing several antique stores. Also in the neighborhood is the interesting Cobb Lane area. The Lane itself is cobblestone and is somewhat hidden by the large oak trees. There are several unique shops in Cobb Lane, but it is most known for the restaurants which have outdoor dining in their courtyards. The Five Points South area is colorful with a vibrant festive atmosphere.

The neighborhood typically hosts three festivals each year, including the Spring Festival in May and the Fall Festival, usually in October. Bands, crafts, and food are offered at these events. Usually there is a New Year's Eve "Dropping of the Ball" at midnight with the ball and thousands of onlookers in the central plaza area.

Of the many complimentary amenities available at the Pickwick Hotel, the evening wine and cheese reception in the lob-

by sitting room seems to be the most popular. The event is hosted by the manager, and guests enjoy getting acquainted with each other. There is even a menu book in the sitting room with menus of area restaurants. Guests can take this time to relax and decide where they would like to dine. This setting exemplifies the warm, friendly hospitality offered at the Pickwick Hotel.

OPEN:	Year round
GUEST ROOMS:	63 guest rooms and suites, all with private baths, phones, TVs, radios, morning newspaper and turndown service.
RESTAURANT:	Continental breakfast, afternoon tea, and evening wine and cheese reception. Restaurants adjacent for lunch and dinner. Bar available, closed Sundays.
CREDIT CARDS:	American Express, Carte Blanche, Diners Club, MasterCard, Visa
RECREATION:	Nearby: golf, jogging, picnic area, tennis, antiquing, art museums, historical sights, theatre, lake, sailing, fishing and boating.
RESTRICTIONS:	Pets with approval.
EXTRAS:	Elevator, valet, handicapped facilities, library, meeting space
RATES:	$68-$88 per room. (Tax 7%)

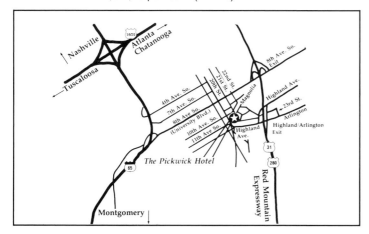

DIRECTIONS:
The Pickwick is located on 20th Street South, in the Five Points South neighborhood, approximately 1 mile south of downtown Birmingham.

**BIRMINGHAM
ALABAMA**

ARCHBISHOP'S MANSION

1000 Fulton Street, San Francisco, California 94117

(415) 563-7872

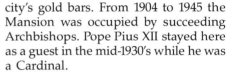

Tucked away in historic Alamo Square, the Archbishop's Mansion is surrounded by some of San Francisco's most photographed Victorian homes. Its close proximity to the Opera House and Symphony Hall make the Cultural Season (September through May) an enlightening time to visit.

A designated Historical Landmark, the Archbishop's Mansion boasts a proud history. It was built in 1904 for Patrick Riordan, the first Archbishop for San Francisco, in the gracious style of a French Chateau. In 1906, when most of San Francisco suffered devastating damage from the Earthquake, the Mansion remained virtually unharmed. During the city's restoration period following the Earthquake, the Mansion served as a refugee center and its vault housed the

city's gold bars. From 1904 to 1945 the Mansion was occupied by succeeding Archbishops. Pope Pius XII stayed here as a guest in the mid-1930's while he was a Cardinal.

In 1980, the current owners purchased the Mansion and began meticulously restoring it. To fully appreciate the magnitude of the project, one must realize that with over 33,000 square feet of interior space, the Mansion was one of the largest houses in the city.

Years of paint, linoleum, and disrepair were replaced with antique furnishings, rich tapestries, crystal chandeliers, oriental rugs and hand-painted ceilings. Special attention was paid to restore the many features that make the Archbishop's Mansion so magnificent including a three-story open staircase covered by a 16 foot stained-glass dome, hand-carved virgin redwood columns, carved mantle-pieces, and thirteen floor-to-ceiling fireplaces.

Antique dealers scoured Europe and the United States for three years looking for interesting pieces to furnish the Mansion. Among the many treasures are an early 18th century carved canopied bed from a castle in Southern France, Noel Coward's 1904 Bechstein Grand Piano, and a large ornate Victorian Pier Mirror that once hung in Abraham Lincoln's Springfield home.

Each room in the Archbishop's Mansion is designed to create an atmosphere reminiscent of the last century. Each guest room has its own flavor, designed to reflect the spirit of a particular 19th century opera.

The spacious Gypsy Baron Suite has an exquisite four-poster bed, with a large sitting area before a baronial fireplace. The Carmen Suite is unique for its huge bath with a freestanding tub before a fireplace. Once the Archbishop's library, the La Tosca guest room is highlighted by a beautiful carved wood fireplace and beamed ceilings. And the Rosenkavalier guest room with its oval bedroom, features a double jacuzzi tub. Many of the rooms feature lovely views of the much-photographed Alamo Square.

Guests enjoy the cozy elegance of down comforters, linens of the highest quality, canopied beds, French-milled soaps and wood burning fireplaces. A basket of breakfast delicacies is brought to the guests' room each morning and wine is served in the Parlour every evening.

The Salon and Grand Dining Room are popular for private business meetings and elegant banquets.

OPEN:	Year round
GUEST ROOMS:	14 guest rooms, all with private baths, phones, radios, canopy beds and down comforters.
RESTAURANT:	Continental breakfast served. No restaurant on premises. Snacks available.
CREDIT CARDS:	American Express, MasterCard, Visa
RECREATION:	Nearby: bicycles, boating, fishing, golf, jacuzzi, jogging, racquetball, sailing, swimming and tennis.
RESTRICTIONS:	No pets, small children not recommended.
EXTRAS:	Elevator, valet, babysitting, meeting rooms, TV's available upon request.
RATES:	$100-$250 per room. Continental breakfast and evening wine included. (Tax 11%)

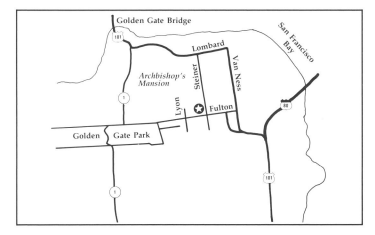

DIRECTIONS:
2 miles from Union Square, in the center of town on Alamo Square.

**SAN FRANCISCO
CALIFORNIA**

DORYMAN'S INN

2102 W. Ocean Front, Newport Beach, California 92663
(714) 675-7300

Romance, luxury, and resounding elegance -- the Doryman's Inn expresses the intrigue of briefly encountering the glamour of a past era.

Enter any one of the ten carefully created bedrooms and relax with the romantic influences of classic Victorian designs. Discover the elegance of fine French and American crafted antiques, and of sunlight streaming through fern-filled skylights, adding highlights to Italian marble sunken bathtubs. Floral draperies and bedspreads, gilt-edged bevelled mirrors, and etched French glass fixtures are all brought to life by a flickering fireplace.

Wake leisurely and find yourself drawn to the parlor for a delicious breakfast of fresh pastries, brown eggs, sliced seasonal fruits, yogurt, cheeses, and the many international coffees and teas. Enjoy the delight privately in your room, or join other guests in the parlor or on the patio enjoying the breezes of the Pacific Ocean. Guests are also invited to relax on the rooftop sunbathing deck.

Located on the Pacific Ocean, the Doryman's Inn is a short walk across the peninsula to the largest pleasure craft harbor in the world. There you can enjoy a vast array of refreshing water activities such as swimming, yachting, deep-sea fishing and wind surfing.

In the evening, Newport Beach boasts over 200 restaurants to satisfy every palate. Dine along the waterfront, and round out the night dancing at a number of the local cabarets.

The early risers should not miss the Dory fishermen returning from the sea with their catch, who for nearly 100 years have supplied fresh fish for sale in the open air market on the McFadden Wharf and Newport Pier area. This area, founded in 1981, is designated as one of California's historical landmarks.

Close by, visit the cobblestone walkways of Lido Marine Village or the Cannery Village and browse through their many boutiques and cafes. The experience of the American Riviera awaits you.

OPEN:	Year round
GUEST ROOMS:	10 guest rooms and suites, all with private baths, fireplaces, phones, TVs and radios. Some rooms with ocean view and jacuzzis.
RESTAURANT:	Over 200 restaurants in area, some adjacent to inn.
CREDIT CARDS:	American Express, Carte Blanche, Diners Club, MasterCard, Visa
RECREATION:	Nearby: swimming, yachting, deep sea fishing, windsurfing, tennis, jogging, golf, sauna, lake and ocean.
RESTRICTIONS:	No pets
EXTRAS:	Elevator, valet
RATES:	$135-$275 per room. Continental breakfast included. (Tax 9%)

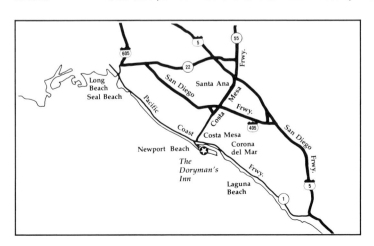

DIRECTIONS:
San Diego Freeway to Exit 55 to Newport. Newport Avenue until cross over Pacific Coast Highway, first signal, make right, one block, make left onto Balboa Boulevard, about 1 mile, next to pier.

NEWPORT BEACH
CALIFORNIA

1-800-533-INNS   **7**

HORTON GRAND HOTEL

311 Island Avenue, San Diego, California 92101

(619) 544-1886

The Horton Grand Hotel in San Diego's historic Gaslamp Quarter is a superbly crafted re-creation of San Diego history and Victorian architecture. Two turn of the century hotels, the Kahle Saddlery and the Grand Hotel have been combined and rebuilt brick by time-honored brick to the original elegance of the Victorian era.

The 1880's atmosphere of the Horton Grand is constantly felt, not only in the decor but also from the period costumes worn by waiters, bellhops, barmaids and chambermaids.

No two rooms at the Horton Grand are alike. Step into your room, and you've stepped into another time; an older, more elegant age of hand-carved armoires, luxurious over-stuffed pillows and canopied beds, delicate lace curtains, genuine antique furniture and, of course, a cozy gas fireplace. The famous guests are as unique as the rooms, including Wyatt Earp, President Benjamin Harrison, Jack Dempsey and Babe Ruth.

Ida Bailey's Restaurant, located in the hotel, was named for the madam of San Diego's most infamous brothel, the "Ca-

nary Cottage", which flourished on the same site occupied by the restaurant today. The food has won numerous local awards and the staff is courteous and caring. The Sunday brunch is the finest offered in San Diego. And today, as in yesteryear, many a gentlemen's agreement is finalized over handshakes and cocktails in the Palace Bar.

On the lobby level is a small Chinese museum. It was placed there because the original hotel displaced an historic Chinese boarding house from San Diego's Old Chinatown district, which thrived before the boom of the 1880's well past the turn of the century. The museum began as a shrine to the boarding house, then expanded to Chinatown in general. It has since evolved into an important showcase that will feature displays from both the People's Republic of China and Taiwan.

Charming horse-drawn sightseeing tours through San Diego's historic Gaslamp Quarter perpetuate the legend of days gone by. San Diego's newest shopping and entertainment center, Horton Plaza, is only a stroll away, and major attractions like the zoo and Sea World are conveniently nearby.

OPEN:	Year round
GUEST ROOMS:	110 guest rooms and suites, all with private baths, gas fireplaces, phones and TVs. Some with balconies. Newspapers delivered daily.
RESTAURANT:	Breakfast, lunch and dinner served daily. Piano Bar.
CREDIT CARDS:	American Express, MasterCard, Visa, Diners Club, Carte Blanche
RECREATION:	On premises: Chinese museum. Nearby: boating, fishing, golf, sailing, ocean, antiquing, art museums, and historical sights.
RESTRICTIONS:	No pets
EXTRAS:	Meeting space, valet, elevator, babysitter, handicapped rooms, complimentary shuttle from airport, turndown service

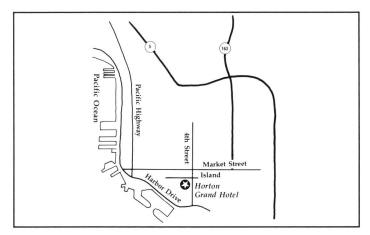

RATES: $89-$236 per room. (Tax 7%)
DIRECTIONS:
I-5 to Front Street Exit, down to Market Street, make a left, then right on 4th Street, go one block to Island Avenue.

SAN DIEGO
CALIFORNIA

INGLESIDE INN

200 W. Ramon Road, Palm Springs, California 92264
(619) 325-0046

The Ingleside Inn is located in the center of the city, and is surrounded by a high white Spanish adobe wall, lovely grounds and backed by the magnificent San Jacinto Mountains.

Originally, the main building was the private residence of the Humphrey Birge family, owners of the Pierce Arrow Car Company. After the demise of Mrs. Carrie Birge, it was acquired by Ruth Hardy, councilwoman in Palm Springs. She was the imaginative lady who had the palm trees installed along Palm Canyon Drive.

Katherine Hepburn and Lili Pons lived here on and off for thirteen years.

The beauty of the Ingleside Inn lies in its atmosphere of calm, peaceful relaxation in the loveliest surroundings. The ambience is of another, gentler world combined with the excellence of European service as it was in pre-World War I days. Each room is individually and beautifully furnished with authentic antiques and such modern conveniences as steam bath, whirlpool tub and small refrigerators stocked with complimen-

Mel Haber's own "BEDTIME STORIES" to amuse and lull you to a pleasant sleep.

If you bring younger children, we have a family condominium building about five minutes from the inn with the same service we render to our main inn guests.

At the inn we have a Halloween Bash - a three day weekend package with a pumpkin cutting contest, and a Fourth of July Bash with a cookout and music. The town offers rodeos, parades, the Bob Hope Classic, and the Dinah Shore Classic golf tournaments. Shopping is nearby in the center of Palm Springs.

Melvyns Restaurant is well-known among business, art and movie world celebrities, and offers continental cuisine which is consistently excellent in a decor that is charmingly old-world. The Patio Garden Room is especially attractive at night, looking out onto a lighted and flowered area that is romance itself.

tary light snacks and cold drinks. The night maid prepares the guest for a wonderful night with turndown service, little chocolate mints on the pillow and

OPEN:	Year round
GUEST ROOMS:	29 rooms, villas and suites, all with private baths, phones and TVs. Some with fireplaces, private patios, and wet bars.
RESTAURANT:	Lunch and dinner served daily. Cocktail lounge.
CREDIT CARDS:	American Express, MasterCard, Visa
RECREATION:	Seasonal: tennis, golf, tram, horseback riding, balloon and helicopter rides, movies, concerts, art shows at famous galleries.
RESTRICTIONS:	Pets by advance notice in some rooms, no children under 16 in the inn proper
EXTRAS:	Valet, babysitting, newspaper. French, German and Spanish spoken. Complimentary limousine service from Palm Springs and Ontario Airports.
RATES:	$85-$500 single or double. Room service, continental breakfast included. (Tax 9%)

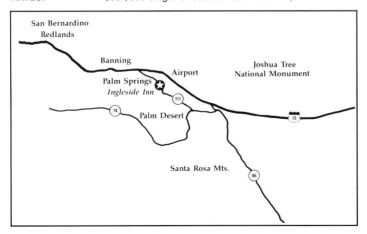

DIRECTIONS:
From Los Angeles, Route 10 to Route 111 (Palm Springs) exit, Palm Canyon Road, all the way through Palm Springs, left on Ramon, Inn is one block on right hand side

**PALM SPRINGS
CALIFORNIA**

LA MAIDA HOUSE

11159 La Maida Street, North Hollywood, California 91601

(818) 769-3857

Though central and convenient to all Los Angeles has to offer, La Maida House is nonetheless considered a tranquil refuge from the hustle and bustle of the city. Between Southern California's mild climate and Los Angeles' cosmopolitan diversity there are plenty of interesting indoor and outdoor activities available year round. The winter months are particularly clear and balmy here in the San Fernando Valley when the California coast tends to be damp and foggy.

La Maida House, established in 1983 by Megan Timothy, is comprised of a main Italianate Villa built in 1926 by Italian immigrant T.G. La Maida, and three smaller California Spanish bungalows built in the 1930's. The tastefully decorated twelve rooms and suites may include jacuzzis, private patios, fireplaces, antiques, and stained glass.

Lunch, dinner and small private parties may be arranged with menus custom designed to your tastes by our award-winning chef. Meals may be taken al fresco in the garden, on the upstairs patio, or in either of the dining rooms.

Guests may also enjoy quiet, complimentary evening aperitifs by the swan pond, in the romantic gazebo, or by the pool.

La Maida House and its grounds reflect the innkeeper's talents as a painter, photographer, sculptress and horticulturist. The 97 stained glass windows, panels, shower doors and skylights are the inn's trademark and were all designed by innkeeper Megan Timothy.

With its location, only 5 minutes from CBS, NBC, Warner Brothers, Disney Studios and Universal Studios, La Maida House is convenient for those seeking the sights or working with the corporate world of the Los Angeles area.

Guests who rise early may enjoy morning tea or coffee and a newspaper delivered to their room in advance of breakfast.

OPEN:	Year round
GUEST ROOMS:	12 guest rooms and suites, all with private baths, phones, radios and TVs. Jacuzzis in some rooms.
RESTAURANT:	Breakfast and lunch served. Dinner served by prior reservation only. Restaurants nearby. Complimentary wine with dinner and in the evening.
CREDIT CARDS:	Not accepted
RECREATION:	On premises: outdoor pool, indoor games, and small gym. Nearby: ocean, antique shops, golf, tennis, jogging and hiking trails, horseback riding and historical sights. Movie studios nearby.
RESTRICTIONS:	No pets, no smoking. Two night minimum stay.
EXTRAS:	Meeting space, German spoken

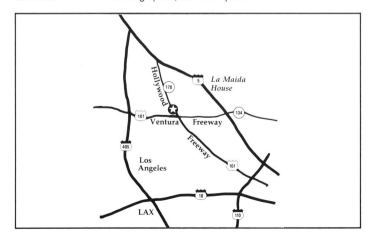

RATES:
$80-$185 per room.
Continental breakfast
and early evening
snacks included.
(Tax 11%)

DIRECTIONS:
From Ventura Freeway
take Lankershim
Boulevard north several
blocks to La Maida
Street on the left.

**NORTH
HOLLYWOOD
CALIFORNIA**

MOUNTAIN HOME INN

810 Panoramic Highway, Mill Valley, California 94941

(415) 381-9000

An elegant country inn situated on the highest mountain in the Bay area, Mountain Home Inn has panoramic views reminding you of the French Riviera. The inn's architecture is Californian and resembles a smaller version of the Grand Hotels of the National Parks. Redwood and cedar are used inside and out.

The inn is only a few feet from the mountaintop highway that takes you to the top of 2,600 foot-high Mt. Tamalpais or to the inspiring coastal highway, to Stinson Beach or Point Reyes National Seashore.

The restaurant is well known for its French and American Regional cuisine. The freshest ingredients are used with the inn growing its own herbs, baby vegetables and edible flowers. Specialties include the freshest seafood and wild game. Wine and culinary special events are offered at the inn throughout the year.

Each of the sleeping rooms is uniquely designed and filled with original artwork and wildflowers. Some rooms have jacuzzis and fireplaces and most have terraces. All enjoy spectacular vistas of San Francisco Bay, the Tiburon Peninsula, the East Bay Hills and Mt. Diablo. Overnight guests have their own dining room and deck at room level. Breakfast and dinner are served there. Lunch may be taken in the upstairs dining room or on the upper deck. Elegant picnic lunches are prepared upon request.

With eight well-marked trails adjoining the inn, Mountain Home Inn is the perfect spot to walk with nature. Across the road is one trail which leads down to the 300 foot tall, 18 foot thick redwoods of Muir Woods National Monument. There are other hiking opportunities in Mt. Tamalpais State Park.

Nearby, in Mill Valley are small communities known for being home to many artisans. Art galleries and boutique shops are fun to browse through on a rainy day. In early fall, you may wish to participate in the Mill Valley and Sausalito Art Festivals as well as the Mill Valley International Film Festival.

For a break from civilization yet only twenty minutes away from San Francisco, the Mountain Home Inn is a treasure not to be missed.

OPEN:	Year round
GUEST ROOMS:	10 guest rooms and suites, all with private baths. Some rooms with jacuzzi and fireplaces.
RESTAURANT:	Continental breakfast everyday, lunch and dinner are served except on Monday. Pub.
CREDIT CARDS:	American Express, MasterCard, Visa
RECREATION:	On premises: walking and jogging paths. Nearby: fishing, ocean, tennis, crafts, theatre, bicycles, sailing.
RESTRICTIONS:	No pets, no children under 6 years of age.
EXTRAS:	Handicapped facilities, meeting space
RATES:	$108-$178 per room. Continental Breakfast and complimentary wine included.

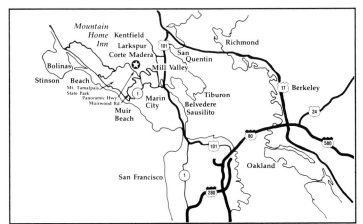

(Tax 8%)

DIRECTIONS:
Take Highway 1 across the Golden Gate Bridge. Exit right on Highway 1 at Mill Valley. After 3 miles (in woods and grassland, past last house) turn right on Panoramic Highway. Proceed 3.25 miles to inn on right side of highway, opposite large state park parking lot.

**MILL VALLEY
CALIFORNIA**

VICTORIAN INN ON THE PARK

301 Lyon Street, San Francisco, California 94117

(415) 931-1830

The mansion has had an interesting history. It was built for a prominant lawyer and legislator, Thomas Clunie, and lavishly decorated with bay windows, stained glass and ornate redwood carvings. This has all been beautifully refurbished. After a half-century of its existence as a private residence it then functioned as a nursing home, apartment house, commune to the "flower children", corporate facility, therapy center and now as an elegant inn.

The Victorian furnishings of the parlour reflect its 19th century origins. The fireplace is carved from maplewood and has its original white tiles. The early Morris wallpaper was reproduced from original designs and is a lovely background to the fringed lampshades, old pictures and velvet drapes. Each of the twelve rooms is different and each reflects its own character. The Clunie Room has bay windows and a large claw-footed tub. The Belvedere Suite opens to a terrace facing the park. It has a small marble fireplace and stained glass French doors leading to a Roman tub for two.

Breakfast is served in the oak paneled dining room with soft music and the aroma of baked breads and croissants.

Late afternoon and early evening are special times at the inn as guests gather in the parlor to share their day's adventures, enjoy a bit of refreshment, or quietly relax with a book in the library.

The Victorian Inn on the Park is a microcosm of San Francisco itself, its history, its social changes and current trends.

The Victorian Inn on the Park, a registered Historic Landmark also known as the "Clunie House", was built in 1897, Queen Victoria's Diamond Jubilee year. In this era of San Francisco's Victorian Renaissance, the owners have restored and revived the essence of the 1890s by renovating this stately mansion. The exterior of the house is still largely unchanged, as is the corner on which it stands. The crowning architectural achievement of the house is the open, octagonal shaped belvedere turret at the very top. This was actually the trademark of its famous architect, William Curlett, who designed many famous buildings in San Francisco.

OPEN: Year round
GUEST ROOMS: 12 guest rooms and suites, all with private baths. Some with fireplaces. TVs and phones available upon request.
RESTAURANT: Breakfast served. Many fine restaurants nearby.
CREDIT CARDS: American Express, MasterCard, Visa
RECREATION: Nearby: bicycles, historical sights, art museums and antique shops.
RESTRICTIONS: No children under 2. No handicapped facilities.
RATES: $75-$200 per room. Continental breakfast and wine in the evening included. (Tax 9.75%)

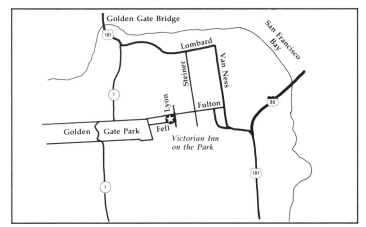

DIRECTIONS:
Highway 101 to Fell Street Exit, continue on Fell Street approximately 2 blocks, turn right onto Lyon, inn is on left.

SAN FRANCISCO CALIFORNIA

HEARTHSTONE INN

506 North Cascade, Colorado Springs, CO 80903

(719) 473-4413

Colorado Springs is nestled against the base of Pikes Peak, at 6200 feet altitude, where the crisp dry air of the mountains has drawn visitors from all over the world. All seasons offer special attractions--the crunch of snow on a sunny winter day, the green and blaze of gold as aspens turn in late September, the enthusiastic outdoor activities of summer in the Rockies, and the thrill of flowers, green grasses and new life of spring.

The wonderful museums of Colorado Springs--history, art, coins, ice skating, wildlife--are open all year. Such attractions as the train to the top of Pikes Peak and Seven Falls are summer highlights, while chuckwagon dinners, Garden of

the Gods Park, the Olympic Training Center and Air Force Academy are open all year.

A special time to come to the Hearthstone might be December--when Victorian decorations and a 20 foot tree heighten the holiday spirit. The 4th of July in Colorado Springs is highlighted by a symphony in the park, complete with fireworks. Labor Day weekend is the time of the hot air balloon festival. Summer is high season, as Colorado Springs has historically been a summer resort, so reservations some weeks ahead are recommended for May to October.

The Hearthstone Inn, listed on the National Register of Historic Places, sits on a large corner lot on a boulevard near the center of town. Flower beds surrounding the building echo the vibrant Victorian colors of plum, lilac, bittersweet and gray which adorn this Queen Anne lady. The large maple, elm and ash trees offer shade and provide homes for the birds and squirrels of the neighborhood. The wraparound front veranda has large rockers for enjoying the breezes and relaxing with a cup of coffee or iced tea.

Each of the 25 rooms at the Hearthstone is uniquely furnished and decorated. Doors to unoccupied rooms are left open so guests may look around.

Breakfast at the Hearthstone is a family style affair. Each day brings some new treat. Always there is a hearty entree, fresh baked bread and a fruit dish.

OPEN:	Year round
GUEST ROOMS:	25 guest rooms, 23 with private baths. Some with working fireplaces and some with private porches. No phones or TVs in rooms.
RESTAURANT:	Full family style breakfast. Several restaurants within walking distance.
CREDIT CARDS:	American Express, MasterCard, Visa
RECREATION:	On premises: jogging and walking paths, picnic area, reading. Nearby: Golf, indoor pool, tennis, antiquing, crafts and historical sights.
RESTRICTIONS:	No smoking in dining room, no pets
EXTRAS:	Meeting space
RATES:	$50-$95 per room. Breakfast included. (Tax 7.7%)

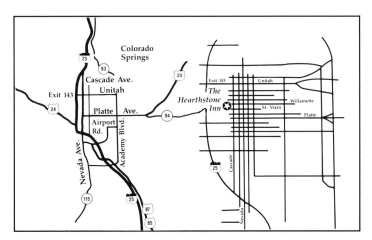

DIRECTIONS:
From I-25, use exit 143 (Uintah Street) travel east to third stop light (Cascade Avenue), turn right. Travel 7 blocks. The Inn is on the right at the corner of St. Vrain and Cascade.

COLORADO ·
SPRINGS
COLORADO

QUEEN ANNE INN

2147 Tremont Place, Denver, Colorado 80205

(303) 296-6666

The Queen Anne Inn, built in 1879 is part of the oldest surviving residential neighborhood in Denver. Thanks to National and Local Historic District designation, a fountain park and a buffer of open space, the neighborhood has retained its quiet character despite being less than four blocks from the very center of the downtown highrises with all their offices, agencies, clubs, stores and restaurants. A pleasant way to travel the distance is by the horse drawn carriages which will come to the inn's front door on request.

All the things most valued by inn travellers are offered by the inn both elegantly and tastefully. The inn features period lighting, quality antiques, fresh flowers, original art, stereo chamber music, gardens, stunning views and sophisticated friendly hosts. The interior decor is warm, light and airy with high ceilings, tall windows and a warm peach tone highlighted in crisp white trim. Despite the unifying theme, each room is dramatically different with various woods and accent colors.

Some of the rooms spotlight pillared canopy beds, some with gleaming brass. Some beds are carved woods. Many are antique, but all have new firm support mattresses.

The overall feeling is that of visiting the home of a well-to-do, beloved maiden aunt. Although the Queen Anne Inn has only been open a short time, it has already been named by local papers as "Best B&B in Town" and as "THE place" for urban romantics. You may arrive as a stranger, but we believe you will leave as a good friend.

The Queen Anne is located in the heart of Denver, commonly described as the Queen City of the Plains. The city of two and one-half million is startlingly clean and safe, with every cultural, recreational and culinary opportunity imaginable. That 200 plus mile curtain wall of those "purple mountains

majesty" can be seen from everywhere in the city, including the inn.

Within three hours are over two-thirds of Colorado's unbeatable ski slopes, golf courses, museums, theaters, shopping centers, restaurants, ghost towns, parks, passes, forests, streams and lakes. Best of all, it comes with the incredible Mile High sunshine, which provides more sunny days than Los Angeles or Miami, and that friendly hospitality, for which the West is famous.

OPEN:	Year round
GUEST ROOMS:	10 guest rooms, all with private bathrooms, air conditioning, personal heat controls, and working area.
RESTAURANT:	There are many restaurants within walking distance. Continental breakfast, along with snacks, soft drinks, coffee and tea are available.
CREDIT CARDS:	MasterCard, Visa
RECREATION:	Nearby: The U.S. Mint, Denver Art Museum, Botanic Gardens, and Mile High Stadium.
RESTRICTIONS:	No handicapped facilities, no smoking, no pets. No children under 15. Must request phone in room.

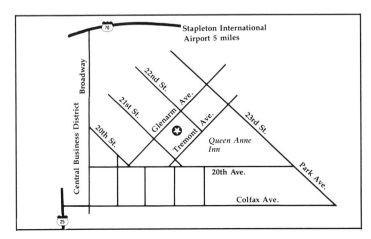

RATES: $54-$99 per room. Continental breakfast included. (Tax 11.8%)

DIRECTIONS: Exit I-25, turn left and proceed to 20th Avenue. The inn is directly ahead across the small park. Turn left and then turn an angle right and an immediate hard right onto the 2100 block of Tremont Place.

DENVER COLORADO

STRATER HOTEL

699 Main Avenue, Durango, Colorado 81302

(303) 247-4431

Surrounded by the majestic San Juan Mountains, the Victorian Strater Hotel in Durango, Colorado has been the center of activity in town for 100 years. This hotel was once known as the finest Victorian Hotel in the west and possibly in the nation. The Strater has a central location for train trips, hunting, fishing, hiking, shopping, art browsing or just relaxing.

Since 1887, the elegant Strater Hotel has held a reputation for fine service and friendly hospitality. Its red brick exterior with whitewood highlights is a focal point of Main Avenue in the center of the historic and entertainment district.

The Strater boasts the world's largest collection of American Victorian antiques. The guest rooms feature high ornate headboards, canopy beds, velvet drapes and hand-carved marble topped dressers.

Winter guests can also enjoy the hotel's new large jacuzzi which is contemporary in convenience yet Victorian in its styling. Many other leisure time activities can be arranged, as the Strater works directly with the famous Narrow Gauge Railroad and a variety of other local attractions. Enjoy golf, tennis, rafting, ballooning or just relaxing in the jacuzzi.

Fine cuisine served with old world

friendly bartenders and saloon girls. The fun loving and warm atmosphere is made complete with live ragtime music performed nightly by some of the country's best honky-tonk pianists.

For over 25 years, the Strater has presented turn-of-the-century productions in the Diamond Circle Theatre, one of the Nation's top melodramas. The authentic melodramas are followed by the Diamond Circle Vaudeville Review from June through September. This fun-filled entertainment is staged by a professional cast from across the country.

The Strater is truly one-of-a-kind. It is the perfect setting for family vacations to the mountains, VIP retreats, conferences, special meetings and romantic rendezvous. Internationally known for its gracious hospitality and Victorian charm, you can be sure of a memorable experience at the historic Strater Hotel.

hotel service can be enjoyed in Henry's, named after Henry Strater who built the Hotel in 1887. The old west lives on in the Strater's own Diamond Belle Saloon, where visitors and locals all enjoy the

OPEN:	Year round
GUEST ROOMS:	93 guest rooms and suites, all with private baths, phones, TVs and music.
RESTAURANT:	Two dining areas, serving breakfast, lunch and dinner daily. Honky Tonk piano bar.
CREDIT CARDS:	American Express, MasterCard, Visa, Diners Club, Carte Blanche
RECREATION:	On premises: live theatre June through September. Nearby: hunting, fishing, train trips, bicycles, boating, cross-country and downhill skiing, golf, and tennis.
RESTRICTIONS:	No pets
EXTRAS:	Meeting space, elevator, valet
RATES:	$37-$104 per room. (Tax 9.2%)

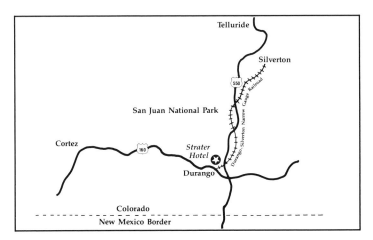

DIRECTIONS:
Follow signs , 1½ blocks from railroad station in Durango.

**DURANGO
COLORADO**

WATER'S EDGE INN & RESORT

1525 Boston Post Road, P.O. Box 938, Westbrook, Connecticut 06498
(800) 222-5901 (203) 399-5901

An impressive turn-of-the-century New England resort, Water's Edge Inn and Resort offers the charm and beauty of maritime Connecticut mingling with sporting activities to delight any enthusiast.

Situated on a sparkling stretch of private beach, Water's Edge Inn offers such relaxing diversions as swimming, sunning or boating. Within the inn's 15 acres of spacious lawns and shade trees, guests can work out at the modern exercise center, play day or night tennis, or swim indoors or out.

Those who prefer more relaxing pastimes will enjoy visiting Historic Essex, known for its Old New England architecture and charming restaurants. Westbrook also has a quaint town center with specialty shops and restaurants.

The restaurant at Water's Edge overlooks Long Island Sound. Serving traditional New England, Continental and Nouvelle cuisine, meals are prepared fresh by one of Connecticut's most accomplished chefs.

Accommodations include both turn-of-the-century decorated inn rooms and more modern style condominiums. Most rooms have a magnificent view of Long Island Sound. At Water's Edge Inn, the rolling surf and gentle waves complete the relaxing experience.

Another favorite pastime is sipping a favorite beverage in the Water's Edge Bar, with it's soaring ceilings, subdued lighting, plush furnishings and unobtrusive pianist.

OPEN:	Year round
GUEST ROOMS:	32 rooms and suites, all with private baths, TVs, telephones and country decor.
RESTAURANT:	Serves breakfast, lunch and dinner. Piano Bar.
CREDIT CARDS:	American Express, MasterCard, Visa, Diners Club
RECREATION:	On premises: exercise center, swimming, golf, tennis, beach, sunning, boating. Nearby: shopping, historical sites.
RESTRICTIONS:	NONE
RATES:	$70-$175 per room. (Tax 7.5%)

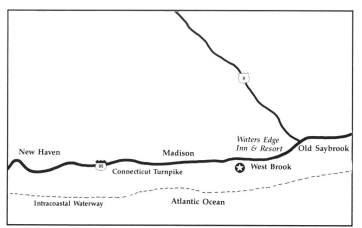

DIRECTIONS:
From North, I-95 to Exit 65, turn left, follow to light. Left ¼ miles on right. From South, I-95 to Exit 65.

**WESTBROOK
CONNECTICUT**

THE CROWN HOTEL

109 North Seminole Avenue, Inverness, Florida 32650
(904) 344-5555

Inverness is a charming small Florida town with an abundance of beautiful lakes and waterways allowing for excellent boating and fishing. The surrounding countryside is still unspoiled and such a pleasant contrast to the big cities. Inverness has a recreation park where walking, jogging, tennis and racquetball are available. Golfers are well catered to at local clubs, and our Crown Hotel has special golf package plans at ten local courses.

The Crown Hotel is approximately 1½ hours from Disney World, Sea World, and all major tourist attractions. Other superb attractions such as Silver Springs, Homosassa Springs and Weeki Wachee are even closer. The Gulf of Mexico is only 20 miles away.

Once a general store in the bustling downtown community of Inverness near Crystal River in Citrus County, the 90 year old inn has been refurbished in the manner of an English country home, complete with an antique double decker bus parked near the canopied entryway.

Unlike many modern renovations, the Crown Hotel has brought to Florida the splendor of the Victorian era, bedazzled

with the famous Crown Jewels and personalized by a conscientious staff, who -- from waitress and waterboy to maid and maitre d' --take exceptional pride in their knowledge of and position with the Crown Hotel. At this guesthouse, you are indeed, a special guest.

The reception area glows with reflections from the glass-encased replicas of the Crown Jewels and framed pictorials of the monarchy. A carved mahogany stairway spirals to the second floor sitting and guestrooms. Each is individually styled with brass headboards, tufted velvet chairs, tasselled draperies, and coordinated bath with ornate goldplat-

ed fixtures.

The Crown Hotel first offered fine food and comfortable lodging in the early 1890's. The vintage elegance of that period has been lovingly restored in first class European tradition for your pleasure today. Each corner of the Crown seems to hold an intriguing treasure. Churchill's is a tribute to dining, offering exquisite cuisine, fine wines, and traditional European service in a crystal and candlelight atmosphere. The Fox and Hounds tavern is a re-creation of an English Pub, complete with polished copper-topped bar and oak floor.

The Crown Hotel proudly offers the Buckingham and Windsor Rooms for special occasions, featuring an extensive array of banquet menus and services. A warm welcome awaits you at the Crown Hotel -- where everything has been designed with the comfort and enjoyment of our guests in mind.

OPEN:	Year round
GUEST ROOMS:	34 guest rooms and suites, all with private baths, TVs, phones. Some with desk areas and radios.
RESTAURANT:	Breakfast, lunch and dinner served. Lounge with complimentary hors d'oeuvres.
CREDIT CARDS:	American Express, Carte Blanche, Diners Club, MasterCard, Visa
RECREATION:	On premises: outdoor pool, checkers/chess, crafts. Nearby: boating, fishing, golf, jogging, walking paths, racquetball, picnic areas.
RESTRICTIONS:	No pets
EXTRAS:	Meeting space, elevator, babysitting
RATES:	$40-$60 per room. (Tax 7%)

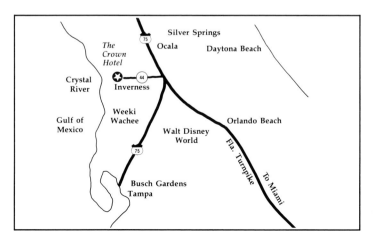

DIRECTIONS:
Located an hour north of Tampa on I-75 to SR44 in Inverness or U.S. Highway 19 to 44 in Inverness

**INVERNESS
FLORIDA**

HOTEL PLACE ST. MICHEL

162 Alcazar Avenue, Coral Gables, Florida 33134
(800) 247-8526 (305) 444-1666

Local residents and savvy travellers have long known about an intimate, European-style inn located in the heart of the Coral Gables business district. Today, more and more travellers are discovering the Hotel/Restaurant Place St. Michel.

Built in the heyday of the 1920s as the Sevilla Hotel, the property has since undergone extensive restoration, yet retaining its old-world charm. Located only 10 minutes from Miami International Airport and close to all of Greater Miami's major tourism attractions, the Hotel/Restaurant Place St. Michel offers business and leisure travellers alike the utmost in personal service and comfort.

Each room in the Hotel Place St. Michel is individually decorated with French and English antiques. Prices include a continental breakfast, morning paper at room door, fruit and cheese basket and fresh flowers in every room.

The award-winning Restaurant St. Michel, featuring gourmet French cuisine and a variety of imaginative dishes, is open daily for lunch and dinner. Breakfast is also served weekdays, and a weekly Jazz Champagne Brunch is offered.

Stuart's Bar-Lounge, located in the hotel lobby, is the latest development in

a phase of major restoration projects at this historic hotel. In addition to its weekday Happy Hour, Stuart's also hosts complimentary wine tasting parties each Monday evening. A warm and friendly establishment, Stuart's features live jazz entertainment on Friday and Saturday evenings.

The Restaurant St. Michel has received many notable distinctions. From perfect escargot and soup a l'onion gratinee to a chocolate mousse and truly creative coffee, guests experience a welcome menage of cuisine, ambience and service. From an extensive wine list, there is a perfect complement to every entree offered. The Restaurant St. Michel is intimate enough for whispered conversation yet grand enough for catered affairs of every kind. Be sure to visit Charcuterie St. Michel offering creative cuisine-to-go for all varieties of moveable feasts.

OPEN:	Year round
GUEST ROOMS:	28 guest rooms and suites, all with private baths, phones, TVs and radios.
RESTAURANT:	Continental breakfast, lunch and dinner daily. Complimentary hot and cold snacks with happy hour. Piano bar.
CREDIT CARDS:	American Express, Carte Blanche, Diners Club, MasterCard, Visa
RECREATION:	Nearby: golf, tennis, outdoor pool, jogging, fishing, boating, crafts.
RESTRICTIONS:	No pets, no handicapped facilities
EXTRAS:	Elevator, valet, babysitting
RATES:	$70-$110 per room. Includes continental breakfast. (Tax 10%)

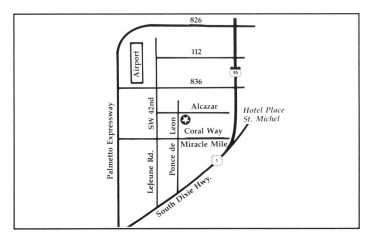

DIRECTIONS:
Hotel Place St. Michel is located on the corner of Ponce de Leon Boulevard and Alcazar Avenue, in the heart of Coral Gables.

**CORAL GABLES
FLORIDA**

1-800-533-INNS **29**

LAKESIDE INN

100 S. Alexander Street, Mt. Dora, Florida 32757
(904) 383-4101 (800) 556-5016

hospitality of the 1920's and 30's.

Operating as a full service resort, the inn offers unparalleled opportunities for vacationers, corporate retreats and lengthy winter stays. Outstanding dining and entertainment are available, making the Lakeside Inn an ideal location for almost any gathering. The Lakeside Inn offers 87 rooms including a variety of suites and parlors. All of the beautifully appointed rooms are showcases for the subtle colorations of designer Laura Ashley.

Dining at the Lakeside Inn is a pleasure all its own, with The Beauclaire Restaurant rapidly being acclaimed as one of the finest of Central Florida. The menu is prepared fresh daily, offering selections such as Almond Duck Lakeside or Chateaubriand du Chef dinner for two.

Each year Mount Dora and the Lakeside Inn host many very special festivals and events, providing guests the opportunity to come and experience an area of Florida that is unlike any other part of the state. The Lakeside Inn also hosts Murder Mystery Weekends, where each guest is able to become the sleuth they always wanted to be. Each mystery is specifically written for the Lakeside Inn, and no two are alike.

The Lakeside Inn offers you the splendor of radiant sunsets, a calming atmosphere of tranquility, and a vacation experience that will live in your memory for a lifetime. The Lakeside Inn is truly the ultimate destination for quality lodging, gracious services, and unparalleled convenience.

Established in 1883, the 104 year old Lakeside Inn is famous as a turn of the century resort and is listed on the National Register of Historic Places. Ideally situated, just 25 miles from Orlando, the Lakeside Inn is the perfect location for travellers looking to see all of the Central Florida attractions.

The Lakeside Inn is one of the most elegant and delightful places one can find with the quietness of a small town, and the quality of service found only in the world's best hotels. Recently, the inn completed an extensive interior and exterior restoration to bring it back to its original English Tudor splendor. To complement the physical restoration, the inn's proprietors are also committed to bringing back the refined traditions and

OPEN:	Year round
GUEST ROOMS:	87 guest rooms and suites, all with private baths, phones, TVs and radios.
RESTAURANT:	Breakfast, lunch and dinner served daily. Lounge with entertainment.
CREDIT CARDS:	American Express, MasterCard, Visa, Diners Club, Carte Blanche
RECREATION:	On premises: bicycling, boating, fishing, golf, jogging, sailing, swimming, tennis, and antiquing. Nearby: theatre and boutiques.
RESTRICTIONS:	No pets
EXTRAS:	Handicapped facilities, valet, babysitting, meeting space
RATES:	$75-$170 per room. (Tax 7%)

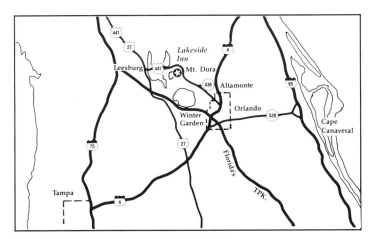

DIRECTIONS:
From North, I-95 at Daytona take 92 west to Deland. Take 44 West. From South, I-95 to Eustis. Turn left at 44B, cross highway 441 into Mt. Dora.

**MOUNT DORA
FLORIDA**

1842 INN

353 College Street, Macon, Georgia 31208

(912) 741-1842

Listed on the National Register of Historic Places and named for the year in which it was built, the 1842 Inn was originally the residence of a prominent Macon citizen, Judge John Gresham, a state senator and Macon's mayor. The main house, which has been restored to its original Greek revival grandeur, shares a courtyard with a carefully restored Victorian-era cottage. Together, these two buildings provide spacious guest rooms, each tastefully decorated and furnished with antiques, fine reproductions, and handmade oriental carpets. Amidst the history, all the modern comforts have not been overlooked.

The 1842 Inn boasts two comfortable parlors where guests are invited to enjoy cocktails and after-dinner drinks from the bar. While guests are dining at one of Macon's many fine restaurants, the inn's staff turns down the beds and places imported chocolate mints on the pillows. Any shoes which are left outside the door are picked up to be expertly shined during the night and returned to the door by morning. A complimentary continental breakfast consisting of pastries, fresh fruit and juice, and tea or coffee is served in the guest rooms each morning along with the local paper and a vase of fresh flowers.

There is much to see and do in Macon. You might enjoy touring the fine antebellum residences and public buildings, or the cultural activites made available by the Macon Little Theatre, Theatre Macon, the Grand Opera house, the Harriet Tubman Museum, and the Museum of Arts and Sciences. The 1842 Inn is located in the center of Macon's historic district. Known as the antebellum heart of the South, the city boasts more white-columned buildings than any other city in the United States. Many of these fine old buildings are within walking distance of the inn, such as the Hay House - an Italian Renaissance mansion, and Cannonball House - the only building in Macon to be hit by Union gunfire during the Civil War. Thanks to its thousands of flowering Yoshino cherry trees, Macon is also known as the Cherry Blossom Capital of the world.

Whether visiting Macon for business, a honeymoon, or just a leisurely getaway, the 1842 Inn is the perfect place to experience the charm and hospitality of the Old South.

OPEN: Year round

GUEST ROOMS: 22 guest rooms, all with private baths, phones, TVs, radios and some with whirlpools.

RESTAURANT: Continental breakfast served in the parlors. Restaurants within walking distance.

CREDIT CARDS: American Express, MasterCard, Visa

RECREATION: Nearby: lake, tennis, antiquing, art museums, historical sights and theatre.

RESTRICTIONS: No pets

EXTRAS: Children under 12 free. Valet, laundry service, turndown service, handicapped facilities, morning paper and shoe shine.

RATES: $55-$85 per room. Includes continental "plus" breakfast. (Tax 7%)

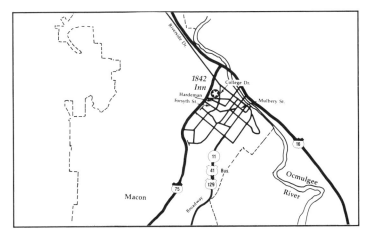

DIRECTIONS:
Route 75N to Exit 52,
Second light to Forsyth,
Third light left on College Street, Two blocks

**MACON
GEORGIA**

FIELDSTONE INN

P.O. Box 670, Hiawassee, Georgia 30546

(404) 896-2262

How naturally this new resort fits into the setting on a Lake Chatuge cove surrounded by the Blue Ridge Mountains. The low-level, two-story inn, constructed mostly of native fieldstone with many windows and a cedar shake roof, is designed in a "C" shape, offering lake or mountain views from every guest room. Enjoy the views every morning next to a fireplace while sipping complimentary coffee.

For an out-of-the-way spot, you would be amazed at all that goes on in those mountains. In the spring, the rhododendron gardens are spectacular, and in the summer people come from miles around to the Georgia Mountain Fair and to visit the antique and craft shops. The alpine village at Helen is a fascinating attraction year round and, of course, the waterfalls and natural formations in the area could content a landscape painter for a lifetime.

Fall foliage tours are unbelievable in beauty as you experience nature at its best. Lake Chatuge is outstanding for fishing and water sports. Winter can be enjoyed on the ski slopes near Clayton, Georgia, Gatlinburg, Tennessee and Maggie Valley, North Carolina. The Fieldstone Room with its open fireplace is a great place to spend the winter evenings.

The guest rooms are luxuriously appointed with deep, rich colors complementing the fine traditional furnishings. Each room has its own private balcony with a breathtaking view of the lake or a magical mountain vista.

There is a swimming pool with a waterfall, lighted tennis court and marina with boat slips, pontoon boat rentals and free docking privileges. A playground for small children is available. There is also a conference room which can accommodate up to 40 people.

The adjacent Fieldstone Restaurant combines the lake and mountain views with floor to ceiling windows. Patio dining with a beautiful view of the marina is lovely during summer months, and picnic lunches delivered to the marina are available. The decor combining the oak paneling and mauve and gray colors complement the magnificent view. The restaurant is open daily and the menu offers American favorites from prime to babyback ribs, chicken, seafood and several Italian specialties. A private dining room is available for parties and wedding receptions.

OPEN:	Year round
GUEST ROOMS:	40 guest rooms, all with private baths, phones, TVs, radios and work areas. All with views. Two fully equipped handicapped rooms.
RESTAURANT:	Fieldstone Restaurant open for all meals, year round except Christmas Day.
CREDIT CARDS:	American Express, Visa, MasterCard
RECREATION:	On premises: boating, fishing, jogging and walking paths, picnic area, sailing, outdoor pool, tennis, crafts, shuffle board. Nearby: 18-hole lakeside golf course.
RESTRICTIONS:	No pets. No alcohol served.
EXTRAS:	Children under 14 free, meeting space, handicapped facilities
RATES:	$63-$70 per room. (Tax 5%)

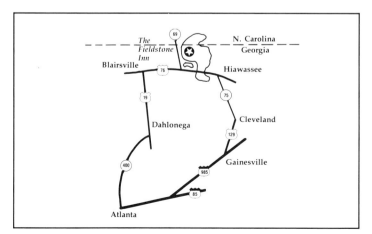

DIRECTIONS:
On US 76, 3 miles west of Hiawassee, Georgia and 3½ miles east of Hayesville, North Carolina. Approximately 2 hours from Atlanta.

**HIAWASSEE
GEORGIA**

THE GASTONIAN

220 East Gaston Street, Savannah, Georgia 31401

(912) 232-2869

Imagine, arriving at a fine historic inn by horse and carriage to find fresh fruit and chilled wine in your luxurious room, or soaking in a porcelain tub with solid gold fixtures and enjoying a complimentary cordial placed beside your four-poster canopy bed in preparation for slipping between fine linen sheets.

The next morning you awaken to the smell of a bountiful breakfast of fresh fruit, juice, quiche, and freshly baked pastries served on Portuguese porcelain and Sheffield silver settings. You may choose to languish in a jacuzzi under the stars, or soak in a whirlpool bath in the privacy of your own room.

Put all of this in one of the finest homes in Savannah's National Historic Landmark District, add unlimited Southern hospitality and historic ambience, and you have The Gastonian.

The inn combines two stately Southern homes, one built for prosperous insurance broker R.H. Footman, and the other for affluent wholesale grocery merchant Aaron Champion. The Gastonian is in the midst of a part of the magical splendor of Olde Savannah. Not intended to be merely a place to stay, it is by design a special place where memories are created. When you enter the door you take a step back in time to experience what it might have been like to live in Savannah in 1868, three short years following the war of the Northern Aggression, the Civil War.

The interior exemplifies craftsmanship of a time gone by: fine woods and heart-pine floors, splendid architecture and design, decorative moldings, brass, ranging staircases, walkways with incredible

views of the historic Savannah skyline. The wallpapers are the original Scalamondre pattern which have graced Savannah homes for decades.

Savannah is a national treasure that features some of the most acclaimed architecture and historical points in the Nation. Its streets are lined with restored 18th and 19th century homes, churches, and gardens, all of which are within walking distance of the Savannah River where English frigates visited these shores two centuries ago. The whispers of yesteryear are whisked away by the whistles from hundreds of freighters, cargo ships and cruise liners utilizing the busiest, and one of the most modern, ports on the East Coast.

The Gastonian offers three parlor meeting rooms with catering for thirty-five to seventy-five. The inn can be rented in its entirety with three to six months advance notice.

OPEN:	Year round
GUEST ROOMS:	13 guest rooms and suites, private baths, phones, TVs. Jacuzzis and fireplaces available.
RESTAURANT:	Restaurants within walking distance. Wine upon arrival.
CREDIT CARDS:	American Express, MasterCard, Visa
RECREATION:	On premises: hot tubs, jogging and walking paths, and library. Nearby: bicycles, ocean, antiquing, art museums, historical sights and theatre.
RESTRICTIONS:	No children under 10 years of age, no pets. Smoking in designated areas.
EXTRAS:	Handicapped facilities, elevator, meeting space
RATES:	$95-$225 per room. Full breakfast included. (Tax 10%)

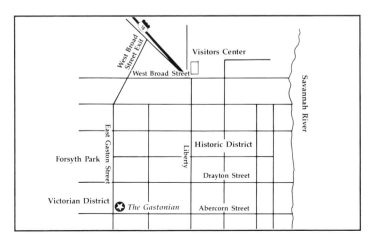

DIRECTIONS:
Take I-16 to the West Broad Street Exit, continue for approximately seven blocks. The inn is on the corner of Lincoln and Gaston Streets.

SAVANNAH GEORGIA

DESOTO HOUSE

230 South Main Street, Galena, Illinois 61036

(815) 777-0090

Galena sits amidst the gently rolling hills of Western Illinois. In the 1800's, the hills were mined for their rich lead ore and brought Galena its notoriety. The entire city is listed on the National Historic Register.

Located on the Galena River and three miles from the Mississippi River, it was once one of the major cities of the west. Galena now remains architecturally intact and steeped in history. Galena provided nine Generals to the Union Army during the Civil War, the most prominent being Ulysses S. Grant. The town boasts 35 antique shops and year-round attractions: Art Fairs, Annual Tour of Homes, Old Fashioned 4th of July, Country Fairs, Mistletoe Ball, Country Christmas, fishing, hiking, golfing and skiing.

The Desoto House was originally built in the early 1850's and quickly became known as "the best hotel west of New York City." The guest register includes such notables as Ulysses S. Grant, Abraham Lincoln, Susan B. Anthony, Ralph Waldo Emerson, and Mark Twain. In April 1986, after an $8 million renovation, the hotel reopened its doors, once again offering deluxe accommodations and superior service.

The hotel has 55 individually appointed guest rooms, two restaurants, as well as banquet and conference facilities for 200 people. The Grand Court Restaurant, which is open for breakfast and lunch, is surrounded by a garden atrium. This is where the Desoto House has traditionally featured its elegant Sunday Brunch. Truffles is the hotel's fine dining restaurant offering American cuisine. The dining room is decorated in the Victorian style of the 1850's.

The Desoto House features package accommodations for all seasons and special events.

OPEN:	Year round
GUEST ROOMS:	55 guest rooms and suites, all with private baths, phones, TVs, work areas and radios. Fireplaces in all suites.
RESTAURANT:	Breakfast, lunch and Sunday Brunch served in the Grand Court. Dinner is served in Truffles accompanied by piano music. Lounge.
CREDIT CARDS:	American Express, Visa, MasterCard
RECREATION:	Nearby: Boating, fishing, jogging and walking paths, outdoor pool, antiquing, historical tours, theatre and art museums.
RESTRICTIONS:	No pets
EXTRAS:	Children under 10 free. Elevator, babysitter, meeting space.

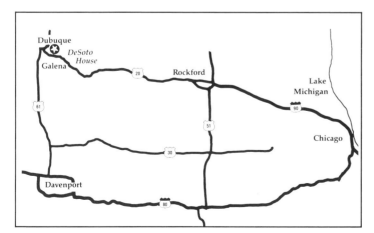

RATES: $50-$195 per room. Breakfast included. (Tax 9%)

DIRECTIONS: Highway 20 to Galena. Go north on Main Street four blocks.

GALENA ILLINOIS

WALDEN INN

2 Seminary Square, P.O. Box 490, Greencastle, Indiana 46135-0490
(317) 653-2761

The architecture of the Walden Inn is unique. Constructed in 1986 on the site of the 1907 interurban and later the bus station, the inn's functional simplicity and gables remind one of Europe. The veranda, wrapping two sides of the building is turn of the century Indiana.

Because it is built on the edge of DePaul University, guests may take advantage of the cultural events and athletic facilities available on campus.

The spacious guest rooms are decorated with soft shades of rose, teal and dusty blue. Much of the furniture was made by Amish craftsmen from Ohio, using cherry, golden pine and light oak.

Irish born innkeeper Matthew O'Neil, also renowned as a talented chef, showcases his creations in the inn's Different Drummer Restaurant. Using locally grown ingredients, the menu features such innovative entrees as barbecued In-diana Black Angus beef medalions with cornmeal fried potato cakes, fanned slices of grilled duck breast in a tart-sweet lingonberry and currant sauce, and fresh cape scallops with saffron cream sauce or fresh dill or raspberry butters. Fresh breads are offered in strawberry, peach, chocolate, banana nut and cherry.

Within an hour's drive of Greencastle are Indianapolis, Terre Haute, Lafayette, Nashville, Bloomington, Brown County and Parke County. All of these destinations offer an insight into Hoosier history and culture. Not to miss sites include the Indianapolis Museum of Art, John Dillinger Museum in Nashville, Elizabeth Sage Costume Collection in Bloomington, Bindley Early Drug Store in Terre Haute and the Old Bethel Chuch in Greencastle.

OPEN:	Year round
GUEST ROOMS:	55 guest rooms and suites, all with private baths, phones, TVs and radios.
RESTAURANT:	Nationally acclaimed, serves breakfast, lunch and dinner. Extensive wine list and spirits.
CREDIT CARDS:	American Express, MasterCard, Visa, Diners Club
RECREATION:	Nearby: boating/canoeing, golf, art museums, tennis, antique shops and historical sights. Bicycle rides, hay rides, and horse rides by prior arrangement.
RESTRICTIONS:	NONE
EXTRAS:	Elevator, valet, babysitting, handicapped facilities, meeting facilities.
RATES:	$61-$125 per room. (Tax 5%)

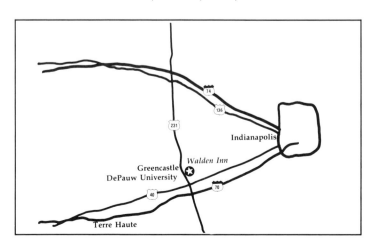

DIRECTIONS:
Take US 231 to Green-
castle, turn west on
Seminary and go 3
blocks.

**GREENCASTLE
INDIANA**

GRENOBLE HOUSE

329 Dauphine Street, New Orleans, Lousiana 70116

(504) 522-1331

Amidst the vibrant joie de vivre of the French Quarter, there stands a quiet 19th century sanctuary called Grenoble House, named after the romantic walled city in France, where the legendary Dauphine family lived. Meticulously restored, Grenoble House is a delicate marriage of classic New Orleans architecture and sophisticated modern convenience.

Three blocks from Canal Street and the chaotic beat of the Central Business District, the world inside Grenoble House is, by contrast, measured and soothing. Exposed brick walls and fireplaces, towering ceilings, and winding staircases strike a fine balance with state-of-the-art amenities for contemporary living.

However, what sets Grenoble House

apart from the ordinary accommodation is that you are master rather than guest, with all the privileges you enjoy in your own domain. Consider Grenoble House your home in New Orleans.

Each of the seventeen suites includes elegant furnishings in a tasteful blend of treasure antiques and smart contemporary appointments with fully equipped kitchens. The sheen of hand-

rubbed hardwood, the gleam of polished brass fittings, the subtle pastels of fine-textured fabrics, are all touches of charming individuality. The plan and decor of each suite is unlike any other.

Customary courtesies are provided as a matter of course, but it is the extraordinary personal attention of the staff that contributes immeasurably to the singular quality of life here. At any moment, day or night, a simple request from you commands immediate action.

A lush tropical retreat. Make of it what you will -- a tranquil backdrop for relaxation, a picturesque setting for an intimate barbecue with friends, or an elegant ambience for a pool side gala. In your New Orleans home, do as the mood suits you.

In addition to overnight accommodations, suites are available on a weekly basis with light housekeeping service available.

OPEN:	Year round
GUEST ROOMS:	17 suites, all private baths, phones, and TVs.
RESTAURANT:	Several restaurants nearby in famed French Quarter.
CREDIT CARDS:	American Express, MasterCard, Visa
RECREATION:	On premises: outdoor pool. Nearby: bicycles, boating, fishing, golf, racquetball, tennis, walking path, picnic area, art galleries and world class shopping.
RESTRICTIONS:	No pets, no handicapped facilities
EXTRAS:	Valet, babysitting
RATES:	$90-$190 per room. Continental breakfast and afternoon sherry included. (Tax 11%)

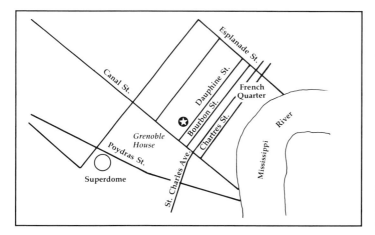

DIRECTIONS:
I-10 to Canal Street, approximately two blocks to Dauphine Street in the French Quarter.

NEW ORLEANS
LOUISIANA

LAMOTHE HOUSE

621 Esplanade Avenue, New Orleans, Louisiana 70116
(504) 947-1161

S ituated beneath moss-draped oaks on the Boulevard Esplanade at the edge of the Vieux Carre, the 150 year old double townhouse now quartering the Lamothe House Hotel exudes Old World charm. It's vintage character and atten- tion to detail transport guests back to the splendor of the Victorian era while providing all the modern luxury and comfort required for today's most dis- criminating traveller.

New Orleans has long intrigued both tourist and business visitors with its combination of Spanish, French and American architecture and history. The "city that care forgot" provides a festive atmosphere year round, particularly in the six by thirteen block area known as the "Vieux Carre" or French Quarter. Here there is a concentration of antique stores, jazz halls, shops and fine restaur- ants second to none in the world. The entire spectrum of New Orleans activi- ty awaits guests as they step through the front door of Lamothe House into the ol- dest quarter of the city.

Lamothe House takes guests back over one hundred years in time to the ambi- ance of a Victorian townhouse residence. No two rooms are alike. The house is built around a classic interior courtyard abundant with semi-tropical plants and banana trees. The decor is mid to late Victorian and each accommodation has a modern private bath. Guests take a classic New Orleans "petite dejeuner" of croissants, orange juice and coffee in the formal dining room under an America gilt bronze six arm chandelier (circa 1840) profusely ornamented with gilded tor- sos, stag heads, verde antico painted putti, bacchanalian masques and a boar's head - truly a Victorian masterpiece.

Of the nine suites available, the "Mal- lard" and "Lafayette" first floor accom- modations have been described as

massive paintings are combined with certain modern touches in the suites to create the warm and cozy atmosphere of a home. Oriental rugs, hand polished hardwood floors and many fireplaces are also prevalent throughout. A few guest rooms in the service quarters are quite small but are furnished and draped in an exceptional manner entirely in keeping with a fine home of the period. In addition to experiencing the city itself, guests at Lamothe House share the individual attention of an experienced professional staff who see that your bed is turned back for your evening return, with a chocolate to clear your palate before retiring. You are invited to sample a fine Dow Ruby Port either as you depart or return from your night's enjoyment. Truly you become part of another way of life in another time when you experience one of the most fascinating cities in the world.

"among the most striking hotel rooms in America." Crystal chandeliers, velvet chairs, ornate lamps, gilded tables and

OPEN:	Year round
GUEST ROOMS:	20 guest rooms and suites, all with private baths, phones, TVs, and nightly turn-down service.
RESTAURANT:	Continental breakfast. Soft drinks and port wine served in the afternoon. Many restaurants nearby.
CREDIT CARDS:	American Express, MasterCard, Visa
RECREATION:	Nearby: bicycles, boating, fishing, golf, walking paths, picnic area, racquetball, sailing, crafts, historical sights and antiquing.
RESTRICTIONS:	NONE
EXTRAS:	Valet, babysitter, concierge

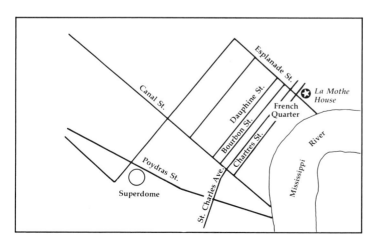

RATES: $65-$85 for rooms. $115-$175 for suites. Based on double occupancy. Continental breakfast included. (Tax 11%)

DIRECTIONS: I-10 to the Elysian Fields exit. Exit from Elysian Field onto Esplanade, continue down Esplanade for 2 blocks to Lamothe House.

NEW ORLEANS LOUISIANA

SONIAT HOUSE

1133 Chartres Street, New Orleans, Louisiana 70116
(504) 522-0570

S oniat House, located in the quiet residential section of the French Quarter, is 3 blocks from Jackson Square and 1 block from the French Market. The Ursuline Convent, the oldest building in the Mississippi Valley, is across the street. The home of Civil War General P.G.T. Beauregard is on the corner.

The year 1829 marked the zenith of the opulent, luxury-loving culture of the French Creoles of New Orleans. It was also the year that the Soniat House was built by wealthy sugar planter, Joseph

Soniat Dufossat, for his large family. Dufossat, brother-in-law of the first Governor of Louisiana, W.C.C. Claiborne, built the house with its iron lacework galleries, cool carriageway, and large courtyard. This courtyard soon became the site for the glittering social life of Antebellum New Orleans.

This same tradition of Southern hospitality continues today. The innkeepers have preserved the historic atmosphere with a meticulous restoration. They have added such modern comforts as tele-

phones and jacuzzis in large new bathrooms, and small color televisions on antique chests.

When seated in the courtyard with its lush, tropical plants, hearing only the quiet trickle of the fountain, it is easy to forget that an exciting city is right outside. In fact, the Soniat House is just a few blocks from Jackson Square, the colorful French Market, the riverfront promenade and America's finest restaurants. Reservations are assured at these restaurants and lesser known bistros due to the expertise of the round-the-clock concierge, who also has extensive information on the city's festivities.

Tours of the French Quarter, Historic Garden District homes, walking tours and museum visits can be arranged. The inn is located just one block from the famous antique shops of Royal Street as well as the smart boutiques, art galleries and jewelry stores of the Vieux Carre.

The French Quarter Festival is held in the middle of April. A jazz festival occurs the last weekend of April and the first weekend of May, and the famous Mardi Gras is celebrated 40 days before Easter. Louisiana is a state of many festivals, and the Soniat has a calendar of all of them and can arrange trips to any one of them.

OPEN:	Year round
GUEST ROOMS:	24 guest rooms and suites, all with private baths, phones and TVs. Some with jacuzzis and private balconies.
RESTAURANT:	Breakfast served in rooms or in courtyard. Several world famous restaurants within walking distance. Reservation service and catering available. 24 hour honor bar.
CREDIT CARDS:	American Express, MasterCard, Visa, Discover
RECREATION:	Nearby: deep-sea fishing, tours, picnic areas, historic sights, museums, antiquing, art galleries and world-class shopping.
RESTRICTIONS:	No pets
EXTRAS:	Valet, babysitter, meeting space. French and Spanish spoken.
RATES:	$100-$135 for guest rooms. $165-$330 for suites. Breakfast included. (Tax 10%)

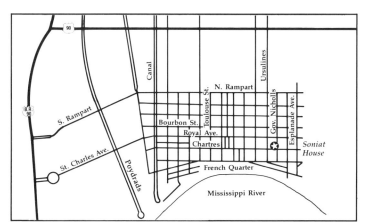

DIRECTIONS:
Leave I-10/US90 at Exit 236A or 236B and go south to Rampart Street. Turn left, go nine blocks and turn right onto Esplanade Avenue. Continue 6 blocks and turn right onto Decatur Street. Go three blocks and turn right onto Ursuline Street. Go one block and turn right onto Chartres Street. Soniat House is on the left.

**NEW ORLEANS
LOUISIANA**

BETHEL INN & COUNTRY CLUB

Bethel, Maine 04217

(207) 824-2175

It was Dr. John Gehring's dream to build an inn on the town common to lodge his patients and other visitors to Bethel. His patients came from the upper ranks of the professional and corporate world for treatment of nervous disorders and the good doctor wanted to accommodate them with the comforts and hospitality they were accustomed to receiving.

In July, 1913, the inn opened its doors to the public. Today, the Bethel Inn and Country Club continues to provide the service and facilities expected of a classic resort.

The village-like Bethel Inn is comprised of five Colonial and Federal style guest buildings, forty townhouse condominiums, a modern conference center, a Lake House, the owner's home and a full complement of recreational facilities.

The combination of traditional inn guest rooms as well as one and two bedroom condominiums offers the overnight guest a unique choice. The guest rooms are individually decorated, with

working fireplaces and the ambience of an authentic country inn. The townhouse units are equipped with modern amenities and are perfect for families and couples who desire more privacy and space. Regardless of the choice of accommodations, all guests have full use of the inn's facilities.

The dining rooms and veranda offer continental cuisine and traditional New England fare, ranging from Yankee pot roast and roast duck to lobster and crabmeat casserole. Dinner is complete with classical music and show themes played on a turn-of-the-century Steinway.

The Bethel Inn and Country Club has fine recreational facilities. The new 18-hole golf course, designed by Geoffrey Cornish, is complemented with a driving range and putting green. A Lake House on Songo Pond offers sailing, canoeing and swimming. Behind the inn there's shuffleboard, tennis, horseshoes and a heated swimming pool. In the winter months, 42 kilometers of groomed cross-country skiing trails are right out the back door. Just ten minutes away there are two downhill ski resorts, Sunday River and Mount Abram. There is also an indoor/outdoor recreation center housing a game room, two saunas, a Nautilus room, jacuzzi and outdoor heated swimming pool accessible from the inside of the building. This wide variety provides a four-season wealth of activity.

Facing Bethel's National Historic District, the inn's buildings on 190 acres seem a million miles away from the hustle and bustle of today's frantic pace. Yet

the town of Bethel is just 13 miles from the New Hampshire border and 70 miles from Portland. With state parks, covered bridges, mountain streams and hiking trails nearby, guests don't seem to mind that the nearest fast food is 22 miles away. Those who prefer to shun the crowds and traffic of the beaten path can find fulfillment in Maine's Western Mountains.

OPEN:	Year round
GUEST ROOMS:	70 guest rooms and suites, all with private baths, phones, clocks, and radios. Many with fireplaces and views.
RESTAURANT:	Breakfast and dinner served in a country dining room. Continental and traditional New England cuisine. Bar, piano bar and terrace.
CREDIT CARDS:	American Express, Carte Blanche, Diners Club, MasterCard, Visa
RECREATION:	On premises: bicycles, boating, cross-country skiing, fishing, golf, picnic area, sailing outdoor pool, sauna, tennis. Nearby: historical sights, antiquing and downhill skiing.
RESTRICTIONS:	NONE
EXTRAS:	Elevator, babysitter, handicapped facilities, meeting space, TV lounge
RATES:	Inn: $56-$91 per person, double occupancy. Includes breakfast and dinner. Condominiums: $104-$224 per unit nightly, EP. Additional $25 per person for MAP. (Tax 7%)

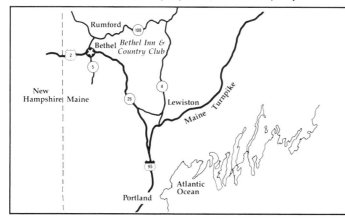

DIRECTIONS:
From I-95 (Maine Turnpike) take Exit 11 (Grey Exit). Take Route 26N right into Bethel and to Main Street.

BETHEL MAINE

THE HERBERT

Main Street, Kingfield, Maine 04947

(207) 265-2000

The Western Mountains of Maine have been a recreational haven for "rusticators" since the Civil War period. However, only in the past ten years have large numbers of people from all over the Northeast discovered the spectacular beauty of the region.

New England's highest waterfall, largest lake, and the Appalachian trail have all been here for eons, but the region owes its recent popularity to the growing interest in skiing, both alpine and cross-country. The Winter Festival occurs during the last week of January, when lift ticket prices are reduced and special fun events take place.

The recent completion of the Robert Trent Jones golf course has added to the summer attractiveness. This, in addition to a lively arts program, has made summer in the mountains meaningful. The summer festival period is from mid-July to the first weekend in August, when the Hartford Ballet and other musical events take place. The other major season is Fall and the "leafer-peepers," from mid-September to Columbus Day.

In the midst of all is the Herbert, since

1918 a gracious oasis in the wilderness. Built by a lumber baron who later ran for governor, the building is late Beaux Arts in style, with handsome marble floors and beautiful fumed oak woodwork in the public areas. A friendly feeling permeates the building and the illusion of entering another place and time is what most first-time guests notice.

The big brass keys, the friendly dogs who welcome guests, and outstanding dining make many guests repeat visitors many times over. The lobby, with its huge fireplace and grand piano, is the scene of many new friendships, both in winter and summer. While many of the guest rooms have antique brass beds, all are thoroughly modern with private baths and spa/steambath units installed for the comfort of the guests. Both the skiers in winter and the whitewater enthusiasts in summer really enjoy this amenity.

After a steambath or jacuzzi, the special treat of candlelight dining from a widely varied menu offers such specialties as quail and native rabbit baked with a sesame stuffing. The wine list, with over 100 reasonably priced selections, is a great surprise.

OPEN:	Year round
GUEST ROOMS:	26 rooms and suites, all with private baths and phones. Thermacuzzi spa units in all rooms.
RESTAURANT:	Dining room open for breakfast and dinner. Lounge.
CREDIT CARDS:	American Express, MasterCard, Visa, Discover, Diners Club
RECREATION:	On premises: sauna, steamroom, masseur. Nearby: skiing at Sugarloaf Mountain, hunting, swimming, tennis, golf.
RESTRICTIONS:	NONE
EXTRAS:	Children 12 and under free in parents' rooms. Local transportation provided.
RATES:	$46-$70 rooms. $95-$130 suites. Rates per room, double occupancy. (Tax 7%)

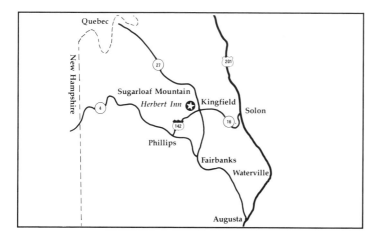

DIRECTIONS:
From the South, take Route 27 off US 1 or I-95 about 1 hour north of Portland. From the East, take Route 2 to Route 27 in Farmington or Route 16 Stratton.

KINGFIELD MAINE

INN BY THE SEA

Route 77, Cape Elizabeth, Maine 04107

(207) 799-3134

The Inn By The Sea offers the luxury of private access to one of Maine's finest beaches, together with proximity to Portland, the fastest growing city in the northeast.

The inn sits serenely on a bluff overlooking Seal Cove, where the natural beauty of Crescent Beach State Park invites guests on the short walk to the beach.

From the moment you enter the inn's marble-tiled lobby, you will notice no detail has been overlooked. One of the main attractions is the 14 John J. Au-

dubon hand-colored engravings that grace the inn's lobby and dining room. These elephant folio Audobons are from a set the artist presented to the City of New York in 1850.

Every room is a suite. In the Main House, Chippendale style cherry furniture complements the in-room bar and kitchen fully stocked with gourmet foods. Luxuries such as a video cassette player, at least two color televisions, telephones and a spectacular view of the Atlantic Ocean pamper all guests. For classic Maine style in wicker and pine,

you may prefer a suite in one of the adjacent cottages.

Meals are served in the elegant Audubon Dining Room.

The Inn By The Sea, with its formal gardens, immaculate croquet lawn with its authentic English Gazebo, tennis court, swimming pool, and shuffleboard court, offers every guest the diversion of his choice.

Portland, a 10 minute drive from the inn, offers fine art museums, two summer theatres, the ballet, a symphony orchestra and an oceanfront aquarium. You could also spend a day at the city's famed old port shops and galleries or along the waterfront where excursion boats wait to take you on a cruise of Casco Bay.

However you wish to spend your time at Inn By The Sea, you will be pampered and able to enjoy the finest Portland and Cape Elizabeth have to offer.

OPEN:	May 1 through October 31
GUEST ROOMS:	43 one and two bedroom suites. All have private baths, color T.V., telephones, stocked bars and kitchens, VCR'S, views of ocean, private deck or porch. Some cottage units have woodstoves.
RESTAURANT:	Breakfast, Lunch & Dinner served to inn guests. Other restaurants close by. Full bar in every suite.
CREDIT CARDS:	Master Card, Visa, American Express, Diners Club
RECREATION:	On premises: Ocean beach, swimming pool, tennis court, croquet, shuffleboard, walking trails. Nearby: Riding stables, golf, yachting, theatre, Portland's cultural activities, shopping.
RESTRICTIONS:	No pets. During July & August: minimum 2 night stay required on weekends.
RATES:	$80-$210 per room, double occupancy. Rates are seasonal and include continental breakfast. (Tax 7%)

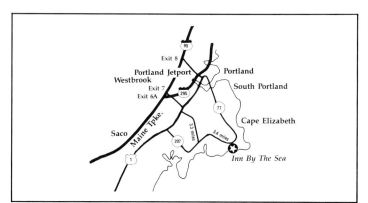

EXTRAS:
Video library, book library with ocean view, concierge, daily newspaper, tour guides.

DIRECTIONS:
Leave the Maine Turnpike (I-95) at Exit 7. After toll booth, take the third exit to South Portland on Broadway to Rt. 77, and continue five miles to the Inn.

CAPE ELIZABETH MAINE

KENNEBUNKPORT INN

Dock Square, Kennebunkport, Maine 04046

(207) 967-2621

The Kennebunkport Inn is located in the heart of Kennebunkport, an historic seaport community, with a busy waterfront and stately old homes. A popular summer resort since the mid-1800's, it offers swimming on beautiful sandy beaches, boating, fishing, golf, and tennis. Best of all are magnificent shore drives and ocean-side walks. During the off-season, cross country skiing on old trolley trails is a popular activity.

Settled in 1692 as Arundel, Kennebunkport became famous in the 19th century as a ship building center. At that time there were nearly 30 shipyards which built and harbored the tall brigs and schooners that carried the nation's commerce.

A Christmas festival in early December is a tradition in Kennebunkport, when the town assumes the character of a Winter Wonderland. The community tree, decorated with painted fishing buoys, is ablaze with lights. The sound of the carolling from the church tower fills the air, as well as the voices of the carollers. The shopkeepers serve punch and cookies, and a festive atmosphere prevails. The inn is at its best on these cold winter nights, serving hot mulled cider before a crackling fire.

Built in 1890 as a sea captain's mansion and purchased in 1926 by Murray Hackenburg, the Kennebunkport Inn has had several renovations over the years. However, the ambience of an old country Inn remains. One of the rooms in the main house has wing-back chairs before a working fireplace, and four-poster beds. During the warmer months, the River House, which is connected to the main house by a deck and small swimming pool, is open. The River House has rooms of various sizes, attractively furnished with some antique and period pieces.

Candlelight dining at the Kennebunkport Inn is truly special. The inn has one of the finest restaurants in the area. Some specialties of the inn are Mustard Ginger Rack of Lamb, Veal Chop with Wild Mushrooms, and Bouillabaisse with Rouille, made like the true Marseille dish.

After dinner, it is a delight to visit the Cocktail Lounge. Decorated in rich, warm colors, with an antique bar, wing chairs and settees, the lounge offers the guest an inviting and romantic spot for a nightcap.

OPEN:	Year round
GUEST ROOMS:	34 guest rooms, all with private baths, TVs and radios. Private phones available upon request.
RESTAURANT:	Breakfast served. Dinner available May - October, weekends in April, November and early December. Restaurants nearby. Lounge.
CREDIT CARDS:	American Express, MasterCard, Visa
RECREATION:	On premises: outdoor pool, sauna. Nearby: bicycles, boating, fishing, golf, sailing, ocean, tennis, antiquing and historic sights.
EXTRAS:	Valet (July and August), babysitting
RATES:	$45-$137.50 per room. Continental or full breakfast included. (Tax 7%)

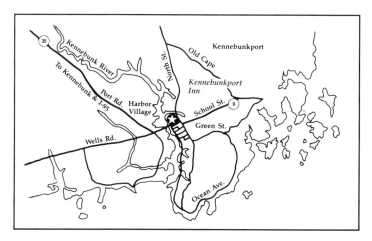

DIRECTIONS:
Route 95N to Exit 2, left on Route 9 (approximately 8 miles). Inn is on left just after bridge and town square.

KENNEBUNKPORT MAINE

LUCERNE INN

Route 1A, Lucerne-in-Maine 04429

(207) 843-5123

The Lucerne Inn sitting high upon a hillside halfway between Bar Harbor and Bangor, is a perfect place from which to explore the many points of interest in the area. The inn is only a few minutes south of Bangor and north of Acadia National Park, one of the most beautiful National parks in the country. Thirty minutes away is the Performing Arts Center of the University of Maine. An hour away is Camden, probably the prettiest coastal town in Maine and one of the very few places from which tall ships still sail all summer long. It's a three-hour drive to Franklin D. Roosevelt's summer house, at Cam-

pobello (open to the public) or to Mt. Katahdin, the second tallest mountain in New England.

The Lucerne Inn is known the world over for its comfortable rooms and gracious dining. Each of the 26 guest rooms has a private bath, wood-burning fireplace, jacuzzi bathtub, heated towel bar, color television, and beautiful view. The restaurant is one of the most popular eating spots in the area, serving expertly prepared American favorites in front of a picture-postcard view. Local residents and visitors come to the inn for its legendary Sunday buffet brunch.

Every Saturday evening a live band

plays 1930's and 40's swing dance music that requires you to hold your partner - music to waltz and foxtrot to. There's always an instructor there if you need to brush up on your technique.

The Lucerne Inn has a fascinating history. Nathan Phillips, fresh from service in the War of 1812, built a house and stable on land granted to him by the government in lieu of a mustering-out bonus. Like most of the land given to those early war veterans, it was pretty useless for farming. Nathan, taking advantage of the fact that he was located on the stage coach route half-way between Bangor and Ellsworth, converted his house into an inn with many gables in which to lodge travellers and stable fresh horses.

While the inn reminded many people of England, foreign visitors as well as Americans who had traveled abroad claimed that the lake and surrounding "mountains" reminded them of Lucerne, Switzerland. In due course, the area immediately around the Inn became known as Lucerne-In-Maine and, in fact, is designated as such on the official highway maps published today by the State of Maine.

OPEN:	Year round
GUEST ROOMS:	25 guest rooms and suites, all with private baths, TVs, phones, wood-burning fireplaces, and whirlpools.
RESTAURANT:	Breakfast and dinner served daily. Also Sunday brunch. Lounge.
CREDIT CARDS:	American Express, Visa, MasterCard
RECREATION:	On premises: outdoor pool. Nearby: Skiing, lake, fishing, golf.
RESTRICTIONS:	No one under 21 years of age. No pets.
EXTRAS:	Meeting space
RATES:	$75-$120 per room. Full breakfast or brunch included. Packages available. (Tax 7%)

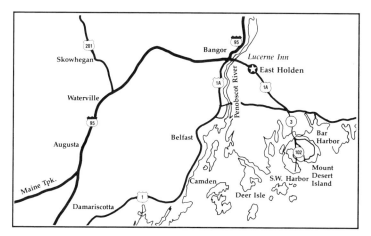

DIRECTIONS:
From I95, take Exit 395 (Bar Harbor/Elsworth Exit) to Route 1A. 7 miles to inn.

LUCERNE-IN-MAINE
MAINE

PHENIX INN

20 W. Market Street, Bangor, Maine 04401
(207) 947-3850

Bangor is the cultural and entertainment center for northern and eastern Maine. Boasting the oldest symphony orchestra in the Nation and, (during the fall and winter months) the Penobscot Theatre Company, the state's only year-round professional repertory group. Husson College and Bangor Theological Seminary as well as the Bangor campus of the University of Maine offer other community cultural attractions. Sport fans find excellent opportunities for both participants and spectators. Five major golf tournaments originate in Bangor and two key New England running events are hosted here. Golfers have their choice of greens at the Bangor Municipal and Hermon Meadows Club, while anglers have access to plenty of action on many nearby lakes and streams as well as at the popular Bangor Salmon Pool.

Bangor offers a headquarters for all season vacations. Indeed, autumn is becoming an increasingly popular travel season since Bangor is so near to the lovely Maine woods whose foliage turns to brilliant colors during this season. Those who would stalk Maine's white tailed deer can prowl nearby woods during the day and return to the city for a relaxing evening.

The famous rock-bound coast of Maine is within an hour's drive for those who enjoy exquisite beauty by day, and a city night life. The Phenix Inn was created from the rehabilitation of an 1873 National Historic Property. It is located in the famous West Market Square block of downtown Bangor. Working within the character of an old commercial building, the inn offers spacious, comfortable rooms in the heart of an old and historic city. The rooms are decorated in a Queen Anne style with all the modern amenities. Breakfast is at your leisure in the second floor cafe.

From the leather furniture of the lobby to the solid mahogany beds of each guest room the ambience of the Phenix is definitely old world.

OPEN:	Year round
GUEST ROOMS:	37 guest rooms and suites, all with private baths, phones and TVs.
RESTAURANT:	Cafe serves continental breakfast. Several restaurants within walking distance. Lounge adjacent.
CREDIT CARDS:	American Express, Carte Blanche, Diners Club, MasterCard, Visa
RECREATION:	Nearby: bicycles, boating, cross country and down hill skiing, fishing, golf, walking paths, picnic area, racquetball, outdoor pool and lake.
RESTRICTIONS:	NONE
EXTRAS:	Meeting space, elevator, valet, babysitter.
RATES:	$44-$68 per room. (Tax 7%)

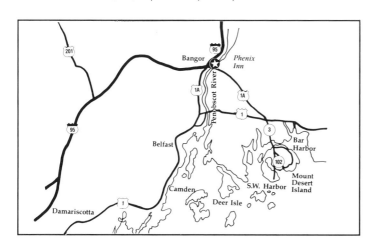

DIRECTIONS:
From I-95, turn onto I-395 to Main Street North. At the sixth traffic light, make a sharp right turn, and Phenix Inn is just behind the small park.

BANGOR MAINE

SHIRLEY-MADISON INN

205 W. Madison Street Baltimore, Maryland 21201

(301) 728-6550

In 1880, when Baltimore merchant Samuel G. Wyman built the Shirley Hotel, the Baltimore Sun described the structure as "a handsome building of modern architecture...of pressed brick with freestone trimmings and terra cotta ornaments". This stately building has remained a hotel, boarding house or inn throughout the years.

The exterior of the Shirley-Madison Inn was described in the 1967 Historic American Buildings Survey as "Norman Gothic: dietetic gingerbread...with gambrel roof, very long windows..." As a guest enters through marble pillars and Gothic stone carvings, the adventure of stepping back into Victorian times fills the senses.

Most of the interior features remain in-

tact, or were lovingly restored in 1985. The majesty of the grand English-style winding staircase of polished oak which looms before the guest in the foyer is breathtaking at its base -- and dizzying at its height (four stories). The century old two person "lift", the oldest continuously operating gas-powered elevator in Baltimore, was an innovation in its day and continues to amuse its occupants as they look through the grille as the floors pass slowly by.

Each of "the Shirley's" rooms and suites are furnished with Victorian and Edwardian antiques, and turn-of-the-century artwork. Charm and comfort are added with brass headboards, plush comforters, cut flowers, and bric-a-brac.

A continental breakfast served in the Morning Room is quite ample to start the day satisfied. When guests return after a day of sightseeing or business, the sherry decanter is full, waiting patiently on the sideboard.

Who is "Shirley"? No one knows. But the best guess is that the name pays homage to the prestigious Virginia family which spawned one governor and several historic plantations.

When the Shirley-Madison Inn was built, Mount Vernon was already one of the finest residential areas of the city. The Washington Monument, erected in 1815, is still the focal point of the neighborhood and is surrounded by diligently restored townhouses and parks. The area is also known as Baltimore's "cultural corridor," with the world famous Walters Art Gallery, the Peabody Conservatory of Music, the Meyerhoff Sym-

phony Hall, and the Lyric Opera House only blocks away. The fabulous, newly renovated Inner Harbor, housing the National Aquarium and Maryland Science Center, is just an easy walk down Charles Street, historically Baltimore's most fashionable avenue of galleries, restaurants and shops.

Guests of the Shirley-Madison Inn enjoy the generosity of spirit that pervades the inn and the charm of a city which respects and has restored its past.

OPEN:	Year round
GUEST ROOMS:	17 guest rooms, all with private baths, telephone, and TVs. Some with kitchenettes.
RESTAURANT:	Continental breakfast and early evening apertif served. Several restaurants within walking distance.
CREDIT CARDS:	American Express, Carte Blanche, Diners Club, MasterCard, Visa
RECREATION:	Nearby: Antique shops, art museums, historical sights. Many things to do in Inner Harbor.
RESTRICTIONS:	No pets, no handicapped facilities
EXTRAS:	Elevator
RATES:	$50-$90 per room. Continental breakfast and early evening apertif included. (Tax 5%)

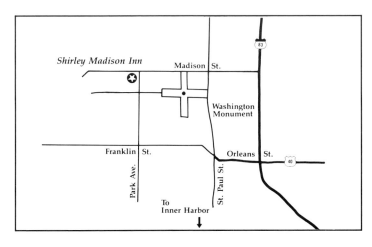

DIRECTIONS:
From South: I-95 north to Downtown/Inner Harbor. Bear right to Martin Luther King Boulevard exit. Right on Mulberry Street, left on Park Avenue, left onto Madison Street. From North: I-95 south to 695 west, Exit 23 (I-83 south/Baltimore). Saint Paul Street exit, south on Saint Paul, right on to Madison Street.

**BALTIMORE
MARYLAND**

ANDOVER INN

Chapel Avenue, Andover, Massachusetts 01810

(617) 475-5903

The Andover Inn is located on the campus of Phillips Academy, one of the oldest and most renowned secondary schools in the nation. Originally built as a convenience for the parents of Phillips Academy students, the inn now serves many other guests, ranging from business travellers, academe and couples who just want to get away for a weekend.

The inn, built in 1930, was a gift of an alumnus of the school by the name of Thomas Cochran, class of 1890. In order to make a place for the Andover Inn, the Harriet Beecher Stowe House was picked up in its entirety and moved by men and horses at a rate of 4 feet a day to the present location right behind the inn.

The elegant dining room is well known for its fine cuisine. Guests dine Monday through Saturday evenings by light classical music performed on the 90 year old concert grand piano. There are close to 60 different wines on the wine list. The atmosphere is one of a large country estate. The lobby is expansive with a large welcoming fireplace, which

is working all winter long. The sofas and wing chairs provide a comfortable setting in which to enjoy the original oil paintings.

The inn has several small function rooms and on weekends these rooms are quite busy with private dinners or wedding receptions. The guest rooms are very cozy and are decorated with an abundance of natural woods.

The activities range from reading a book in the lobby or on the porch, to playing tennis on campus or taking "a walking tour of the campus." There is a bird sanctuary next door and the Addison Art Gallery is across the street. The Academy also has an archaeology building called the Peabody Museum.

In North Andover the Textile Museum is a must see. The history of the Merrimack Valley with mill cities like Lawrence, Lowell and Haverhill is shown there in detail. The National Park in Lowell, 20 minutes from the inn, is also an interesting attraction.

The equestrian shop in North Andover caters to you with horse rentals and trail rides. Box lunches are available at the inn to enjoy during your day trips away.

The location of the inn makes it ideal for seminars, meetings and conferences. A quiet weekend stay when the work is done is popular with conference guests.

OPEN:	Year round
GUEST ROOMS:	33 guest rooms and suites, most with private baths. All with phones, TVs, radios and work areas.
RESTAURANT:	Breakfast, lunch and dinner served daily except lunch on Saturdays. Restaurants nearby. Spirits in restaurant only.
CREDIT CARDS:	American Express, Carte Blanche, Diners Club, MasterCard, Visa
RECREATION:	Nearby: bicycling, cross-country skiing, jogging, theatre, tennis, and art museums.
RESTRICTIONS:	Small pets only, no handicapped facilities.
EXTRAS:	Meeting space, elevator, dry cleaning, babysitting and limousine service.
RATES:	$61-$110 per room. (Tax 5.7%)

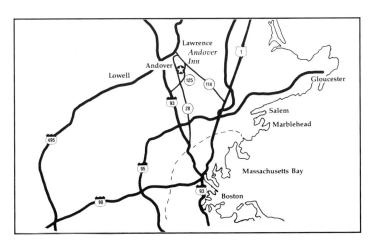

DIRECTIONS:
Located 25 miles north of Boston on Route 28, near the intersection of Interstate Routes 93 and 495.

**ANDOVER
MASSACHUSETTS**

YANKEE CLIPPER INN

Box 2399, 96 Granite Street, Rockport, Massachusetts 01966

(617) 546-3407

Rockport has been an artist's colony for more than forty years. This quiet fishing village was "discovered" by artists during the depression period. And with the artists came the tourists. Today, the salty sea air and the arts and crafts make Rockport, just 40 miles north of Boston, a popular retreat.

In 1946 Fred and Lydia Wemyss bought a lovely ocean front mansion in Rockport. They named their home "the Yankee Clipper Inn" and opened it to

guests. Now their daughter and son-in-law, Barbara and Bob Ellis, manage the inn.

The Yankee Clipper is in a residential area and is ideal for those who prefer a non-commercial atmosphere. The inn consists of three converted private estate buildings. The main building, the Inn, includes luxurious suites with fine ap-

pointments, antique furnishings, some canopy beds, glass-enclosed porches and a main dining room overlooking the ocean.

The Quarterdeck features guestrooms with unsurpassed views of the ocean through large picture windows so close to the water you feel that you are at sea. A landlubber cruise with all the ocean and none of the motion.

The Bulfinch House is more distant from the ocean. Here you will find all the comforts of home set in a classic 19th century New England house of Clipper Ship days with period furnishings.

A stroll through quiet paths, through the town's shops or down by the water is a popular pastime. Many guests also enjoy the heated, salt water pool.

The grounds of the Yankee Clipper are extensive and include the finest ocean frontage on the rock-bound coast of Cape Ann.

OPEN:	Year round
GUEST ROOMS:	28 guest rooms and suites, all with private baths. All rooms have views. TV rooms and lounges for gathering in all buildings.
RESTAURANT:	Breakfast, lunch and dinner served, seasonal. Check when making reservations. Wine may be brought by guests.
CREDIT CARDS:	NONE
RECREATION:	On premises: pool, swimming, fishing, water sports. Nearby: golf, boating, swimming, shopping, art galleries, antiquing, fishing, historical sites.
RESTRICTIONS:	Minimum stay on weekends and holidays. No smoking cigars or pipes. No smoking in main dining room. No pets. No children under 3 years of age. No hard liquor allowed.
RATES:	$48-$85 per person MAP spring and fall. $58-$87 per person AP summer. 15% gratuity. (Tax 5.7%)

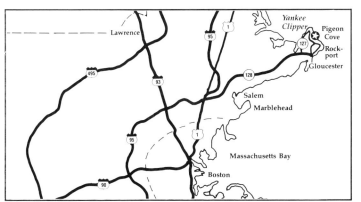

DIRECTIONS:
Follow State Route 128 northeast to Cape Ann where it ends at the first set of traffic lights. Turn left onto Route 127. Go about four miles to where Route 127 turns sharp left to Pigeon Cove. One and one-half miles farther along this road is the Yankee Clipper.

**ROCKPORT
MASSACHUSETTS**

LOWELL INN

102 North 2nd Street, Stillwater, Minnesota 55082
(612) 439-1100

The Lowell Inn of today stands on the site of the stately Sawyer House erected in 1848, some ten years before Minnesota achieved statehood. The Sawyer House of that long ago day brought the "civilized" East to the Frontier. But as more and more of the East's modernity came to the West, the Sawyer House became an anachronism. It fell to the wreckers' ball in 1924.

In 1930, a new Williamsburg style hotel, the Lowell Inn, rose in its place. Today the Palmer family, owners and innkeepers, have recreated the aura of a long ago and gracious era.

The inn's remodeled guest rooms create intimate boudoirs with state-of-the-art bathing facilities. On each satin-quilted oversized bed, there snoozes a small ceramic cat.

The inn is located in the heart of historic Stillwater (one of Minnesota's earliest settlements) on a hillside two blocks from the St. Croix River. The Wil-liamsburg style red-brick building fronts thirteen white pillars to represent the thirteen original colonies. The three dining rooms at the inn each offer a unique expression of the inn's heritage and a love of nature.

The Garden Room's inspiration is a natural outdoor spring which collected into brook trout pools. In 1939, these pools, from which guests would choose their entree, began seeping into the dining room. The obvious solution was to move the trout pool indoors.

The George Washington Room reflects the feelings of Nelle Palmer, Stillwater's Matriarch. Her appreciation and love for antiques from the "Williamsburg Colonial" period echo the Colonial American theme of the room.

Visiting Stillwater is a trip back in history itself. Many of the buildings are listed on the National Register of Historical Sites. Don't miss the Lumberjack Festival in July or the Apple Festival in October.

OPEN:	Year round
GUEST ROOMS:	21 guest rooms and suites, all with private baths and phones. Suites have a jacuzzi bath and small selection of liquor.
RESTAURANT:	3 dining rooms: the Matterhorn Room, the George Washington Room and the Garden Room. Breakfast, lunch and dinner served. Lounge available.
CREDIT CARDS:	NONE
RECREATION:	Nearby: boating, fishing, cross country and downhill skiing, golf, jogging, walking paths, picnic, racquetball and sailing, tennis and historical sights.
RESTRICTIONS:	No handicapped facilities in guest rooms.
RATES:	$79-$139 per room. (Tax 6%)

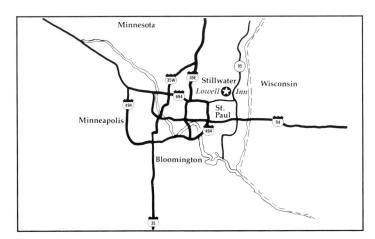

DIRECTIONS:
10 miles from Highway 94, highway runs into downtown Stillwater.

STILLWATER
MINNESOTA

CEDAR GROVE MANSION INN

2200 Oak Street, Vicksburg, Mississippi 39180
(800) 862-1300, (601) 636-1605

Vicksburg, situated on the Mississippi River is famous for the battle of Vicksburg which took place during the Civil War. There is a National military park which is visited by a million visitors per year. The region is popular for it's antebellum mansions and historic buildings. Added attractions are river boat rides, museums, and fine dining.

Cedar Grove is one of the grandest and finest mansions in the state. Built by John A. Klein as a wedding present to his bride, they brought back many architectural amenities from their European honeymoon.

Overnight guests are greeted by the friendly staff as they begin to experience the splendor of the South in the "Gone With The Wind" fashion. The restored mansion has flickering gas light chandeliers, beautiful original antiques and canopied beds. Guests experience the grandeur of the antebellum era with a tour of the mansion and its fine antiques, and a stroll through the gardens with gazebos, fountains, and courtyards.

Four acres of formal gardens, gazebos, courtyards, a swimming pool with spa, a terrace overlooking the Mississippi River, special mint juleps and a Southern breakfast all make your visit a lifetime memory.

The mansion, built in 1840, survived the ravages of the Civil War. It still has a cannon ball lodged in the parlor wall. General Sherman and Jefferson Davis along with many dignitaries of the period visited and danced in the ballroom of the Mansion prior to the War.

OPEN:	Year round
GUEST ROOMS:	17 guest rooms and suites, all with private baths, TVs. 24 hour phone service available.
RESTAURANT:	Full plantation breakfast served. Fine dining nearby. Lounge.
CREDIT CARDS:	MasterCard, Visa
RECREATION:	On premises: Shuffle board, walking path, outdoor pool, jacuzzi. Nearby: antiquing, tennis.
RESTRICTIONS:	No pets
EXTRAS:	Meeting space, tour of the Mansion
RATES:	$65-$105 per room. Includes plantation breakfast. (Tax 7%)

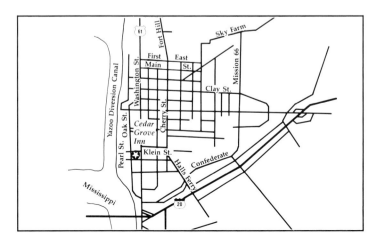

DIRECTIONS:
40 miles from Jacksonville, Route 20 to Washington Street (Exit 1A) to 2200 Block, west on Klein Street

**VICKSBURG
MISSISSIPPI**

INN AT THORN HILL

Thorn Hill Road, Jackson Village, New Hampshire 03846
(603) 383-4242

Your visit to the Inn at Thorn Hill begins by passing through the "Honeymoon" covered bridge on the way to Thorn Hill Road in quaint Jackson Village. You feel exhilarating mountain air and view majestic beauty in the heart of the White Mountain National Forest. Located on a knoll, the Inn is surrounded by the White Mountains which offer a wide variety of recreational activities including hiking, climbing, skiing, fishing and just plain absorbing.

The winter season offers doorstep access from the inn to the 146K cross country ski trail network of the Jackson Ski Touring Foundation (one of the four best in the world!). Alpine skiing is available at four mountains within 10 minutes of the inn. Toboganning, sleigh rides, ice skating, Winterfest and other outdoor activities for everybody make this season very special. Spring skiing at Tuckerman's Ravine is for the skiier wanting the ultimate challenge.

Summer in the Mt. Washington Valley is filled with activities including Arts Jubilee events - concerts, plays and dance troupes, the Equine Classic at Attitash, the plentiful activities of the National Forest, as well as tennis, golf and swimming. There are several county fairs held during the summer with one of the largest in New England climaxing the season at nearby Fryeburg, Maine.

Fall foliage in the White Mountains is spectacular with brilliant hues of red, orange and yellow.

Year-round shopping is enjoyable at the factory outlets and antique shops in Jackson Village and nearby North Conway.

The inn was designed and built by Stanford White, the well known architect, in 1895. The Main Inn and Carriage House have been carefully restored to their turn-of-the-century style and capture the flavor and ambience of the Victorian era. Jackson Village has long been a favorite resort area, and the Inn at Thorn Hill shares that rich heritage. Guests may relax on the porch in New England rocking chairs or snuggle by fireplaces in common areas. The antique-filled guest rooms offer a welcome retreat after a few pleasant hours in the pub, dining room, parlor or the expansive drawing room with breathtaking views of the White Mountains.

The creative cuisine makes a visit to Thorn Hill a special culinary and romantic experience. The imaginative epicurean delights are devised fortnightly to present meals fresh and proper to the season for maximum pleasure. A well-rounded offering from beef and veal to seafood, poultry and game is artistically presented. Freshly baked breads complement the "start from scratch" cuisine with fresh herbs and vegetables.

The complete "Inngoing" experience is fulfilled with the hospitality of the LaRose family, who take every step to make your stay at the Inn at Thorn Hill enjoyable and complete.

OPEN:	Year round
GUEST ROOMS:	20 guest rooms, all with private baths. 10 rooms in Main Inn, 7 in the Carriage House and 3 private cottages on the grounds.
RESTAURANT:	Full breakfast and dinner included. Reservations requested. Pub room.
CREDIT CARDS:	American Express, MasterCard, Visa
RECREATION:	On premises: cross country skiing, jogging, picnic area, outdoor pool, shuffle board, reading. Nearby: boating, downhill skiing, tennis, swimming, golf and more.
RESTRICTIONS:	No pets, no children under 12 years
EXTRAS:	Meeting space
RATES:	$65-$80 per person, MAP double occupancy. (Tax 7%)

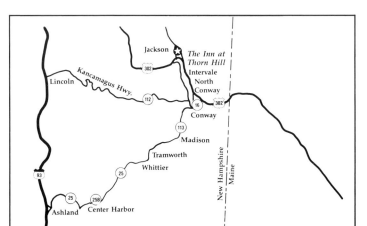

DIRECTIONS:
Leave I-93 at Exit 24 and go east to Ashland. Follow US 3 and State Route 25 and 25B east to Center Harbor. Continue on 25 to Whittier. Turn left on State Route 113 and continue to State Route 16. Turn left and follow State Route 16 to Jackson.

JACKSON NEW HAMPSHIRE

LAMIE'S INN AND TAVERN

490 Lafayette Road, Hampton, New Hampshire 03842
(603) 926-0330

L amie's Inn was once the Lane Family homestead and for four generations the Lane Family home was a welcome landmark to weary travellers on the Olde Boston Post Road. Purchased in 1928 by Albert and Madeline Lamie, the inn underwent extensive renovations, not the least of which involved raising and turning the building to face Lafayette Road.

The Tavern decor is representative of the Colonial style of the original Lane Homestead. Each of the 31 guest rooms have been authentically restored, right down to the hand-stenciled walls, brass lamps, solid cherry furniture, counterpaned and canopied beds. Much of the paneling came from the old Ashcroft estate and the wagon wheels used for light fixtures came from the adjacent field.

For more than thirty years, Lamie's Inn and Tavern was owned and operated by the Dunfey Family, famous as the New England hoteliers who built their family business into the international concern known as Omni Hotels.

Lamie's Inn and Tavern, now independently managed, continues to offer gracious hospitality in the best tradition of excellence and quality service.

Lamie's Tavern boasts an unequalled reputation for hearty native fare. Breakfast, lunch and dinner are served in the Tavern Dining Room. A special Family Sunday Dinner Menu is offered. Express Lunch and Dinner Menus are served in the Lounge on weekdays.

Hampton Beach on the blue Atlantic Ocean is 2 miles away. Sightseers will revel in the historic sites of downtown Portsmouth, Newburyport, the Waterfronts and Strawbery Banke.

Theatre-by-the-Sea, the Hampton Playhouse and Casino, Greyhound and Thoroughbred racing are minutes away. An hour's drive will take you to the Lakes Region and the White Mountains for some of the best sightseeing, skiing, winter or summer sports anywhere in the Northeast.

Special attractions in the area include outlet and discount shopping, Christmas Crafts Fairs, autumn apple picking, cross-country skiing.

OPEN:	Year round
GUEST ROOMS:	31 guest rooms and suites, all with private baths, TVs, phones, and sitting area.
RESTAURANT:	Breakfast, lunch and dinner served daily. Lounge with light fare.
CREDIT CARDS:	American Express, Diners Club, MasterCar, Visa
RECREATION:	Nearby: bicyles, cross-country skiing, fishing, golf, racquetball, sailing, ocean, tennis, crafts, historical sights and antiquing.
RESTRICTIONS:	No pets
EXTRAS:	Valet, handicapped facilities, meeting space.
RATES:	$62-$165 per room. (Tax 7%)

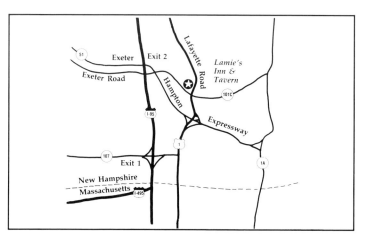

DIRECTIONS:
Leave Interstate 95 at Exit 1, Route 107, follow it east to Route 1, North. Lamie's Tavern is on Route 1 where it intersects with Exeter Road in Hampton Center.

**HAMPTON
NEW HAMPSHIRE**

INN AT MILLRACE POND

P.O. Box 359, Route 519, Hope, New Jersey 07844

(201) 459-4884

The Inn at Millrace Pond is situated on 23 acres along Beaver Brook in historic Hope, New Jersey. Founded in 1769 by Moravian pioneers, this tiny village is listed on the State and National Registers of Historic Sites. Outstanding examples of their architecture remain and may be viewed on the Historical Society's self-guided walking tour.

Just an hour west of New York City the inn commands a central location for exploring New Jersey's scenic Skylands Region, an endless selection of spring and fall craft festivals and antique shows, Waterloo Village, Waterloo's Summer Music Festival, and winter sports in the nearby Poconos. Local wineries offer daily tours. Harvest Weekends are fun during Foliage time. June's Strawberry Festival, Hope's July Antiques show, July Raspberry Trail, and early December Christmas Market are annual events.

Restored to colonial grandeur, this historic inn offers a splendid variety of accommodations. Individually decorated guestrooms in The Millrace House and Wheelwright's Cottage reflect the quiet elegance once found in fine homes of Colonial America. Distinctive antique furnishings, wide board flooring and oriental rugs heighten the feeling of colonial authenticity. Handcrafted country furniture, simple braided rugs and exposed beams underscore the industrial roots of rooms in the Circa 1769 Grist Mill. Modern amenities and generously sized beds have been added for comfort.

The restored Moravian Grist Mill also houses an exciting American restaurant whose interior decor preserves the mill's rich industrial heritage. Guests enter into the original millrace chamber complete with running water. This suggests days past when water power turned the mill wheel to grind local grain. Stone walls, gleaming chandeliers and Windsor chairs accent the formal dining room where candlelight showcases the exposed post and beam construction. An open staircase, descending into the former wheel chamber, leads to the Colonial Tavern where guests can relax on an antique wooden settle before the welcoming fire.

The seasonal menu features American

cuisine highlighted by colonial ingredients. A recent reviewer recommended the American Goat Cheese in Puff Pastry, Corn and Mussel Chowder, Roast Half Duckling accompanied by Apples and a Peppercorn Sauce, New York Sirloin garnished with grilled vegetables and a two mustard sauce, and locally raised Breast of Free Range Chicken.

An extensive, predominantly American wine list suggests California Chardonnays, Merlots, Cabernet Sauvignons or Washington Pinot Noirs and Rieslings to accompany your meal.

Whether you visit the restaurant for fine American fare or linger overnight as a lodging guest, your time at the Millrace Pond will be a special experience of hospitality, gracious service, fine food and spirits and comfortable lodging.

OPEN:	Year round
GUEST ROOMS:	16 guest rooms and suites, all with private baths and radios. Phones available in some rooms. Some rooms with whirlpools and fireplaces.
RESTAURANT:	Dinner served nightly except Monday. Lunch is available at nearby restaurants. Tavern.
CREDIT CARDS:	American Express, MasterCard, Visa
RECREATION:	Nearby: Winery, boating, cross country and downhill skiing, fishing, golf, whirlpools, jogging, picnic areas, tennis, antiquing and crafts.
RESTRICTIONS:	No pets
EXTRAS:	Meeting space
RATES:	$55-$95 per room. Continental Breakfast included. (Tax 6%)

DIRECTIONS:
Route 80 to Exit 12, Route 521 South approximately 1 mile to blinker light in Hope, Left on Route 519 2/10 mile to sign and parking.

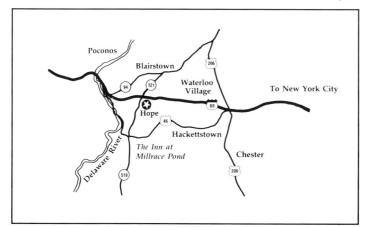

HOPE
NEW JERSEY

THE GENESEE COUNTRY INN

948 George Street, P.O. Box 340, Mumford, New York 14511

(716) 538-2500

The Genesee Country Inn is nestled on six quiet secluded acres in the Village of Mumford. The area was settled in 1799 by Scotsmen. In 1833 Philip Garbutt purchased the land and established a plaster mill, later used in the manufacture of hubs and wheel spokes. Early in the 1900's the Mill was sold to the Gardner Paper Company who built onto the structure, and the Mill became the residence for the plant manager.

Now the old mill has been painstakingly revitalized creating a most comfortable country inn. The charm of the 19th century abounds in the 18-room building with its nine guest rooms and ample common rooms.

During renovation the interior was painted a fresh white which became a canvas for the innkeeper and two local artists who spent nearly three months stenciling their way through the inn. The result is more than historical accuracy. Guests particularly enjoy the MacKay room stenciled in a theme of hearts and swags of pale blues and beige, with its large canopied bed and creme ruffled colonial curtains. All of the guest rooms are tastefully furnished with antiques and reproductions. Each of the guest rooms includes special amenities and a quiet sitting area in which to relax.

Hospitality is a specialty of the inn. Upon arrival, guests are greeted at the door and invited into the formal parlor to enjoy afternoon tea, and crackers and cheese. For dinner, there is a choice of seven fine local restaurants, menus are

on hand, and reservations are gladly arranged by the innkeeper. The inn also has several special dinner packages available. A limousine is available to take guests to dine at the nearby Ganson Inn.

Adjacent to the parlor, overlooking the lovely Spring Creek, ducks, and gardens, is the many windowed breakfast room. A full country breakfast and a bottomless pot of coffee or tea are served fresh each morning.

Less than a mile from the inn is the Genesee Country Village and Museum, 125-acres depicting life in the 19th century in New York State. The village offers a continuing calendar of events for weekends from mid-May through October. Some of these include a Highland Gathering, a Fiddler's Fair, Carriage Marathon and dressage competitions, a re-creation (July 4th) of the Battle of Gettysburg, and an Agricultural Fair in the fall during color season.

OPEN:	Year round
GUEST ROOMS:	9 guest rooms with air conditioning, TVs, phones, and clock-radios.
RESTAURANT:	Dinner packages at local restaurants are available.
CREDIT CARDS:	American Express, MasterCard, Visa, Diners Club
RECREATION:	On premises: Bicycling, cross country skiing, jogging and walking paths, picnic area, outdoor pool, lake and library. Nearby: golf and antiquing.
RESTRICTIONS:	No pets, no children under 12 on weekends. Minimum stay some weekends.
EXTRAS:	Meeting Space
RATES:	$75-$115 per room. Breakfast and afternoon tea included. (Tax 10%)

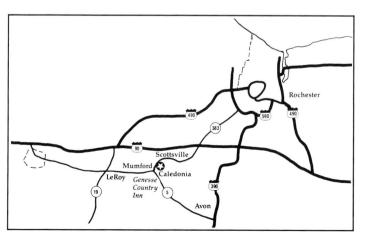

DIRECTIONS:
From Interstate 90, the New York State Thruway, take Exit 47 and North Road to State Route 36. Continue into Mumford. Turn right at the first traffic light onto George Street. The sixth building on the right.

**MUMFORD
NEW YORK**

GENEVA ON THE LAKE

1001 Lochland Road, Geneva, New York 14456

(315) 789-7190

Geneva on The Lake is a small, elegant, four seasons resort in the heart of New York State's Finger Lakes Wine district. This European-style vacation resort is a diminutive replica of the imposing Villa Lancellotti, a well-known Italian Renaissance Villa in the hills outside of Rome. It was built in 1911 by the wealthy Nesters as their family estate, perched on a bluff above the crystal-clear waters of Seneca Lake. The Capuchin Fathers used it as a monastery prior to a complete renovation in 1980 by the Schickel family. Following the renovation, this beautiful and unique resort was placed on the National Register of Historic Places.

Its enchanting ten acres include a terrace, magnificent formal gardens, a grand 70-foot lake side swimming pool, secluded nooks, naturally landscaped paths and a boathouse and dock with sailboats, windsurfers and canoes for rental. Skiing, golf and tennis are nearby.

There are no rooms, only suites, each one individually decorated in classic style. Most are furnished in Stickley antique reproductions. The Classic Suite has two bedrooms, two fireplaces, a canopied bed, balcony, a magnificent view of the lake and a ready kitchen. Guests are greeted with fresh flowers, fruit, and a complimentary bottle of New York State wine on arrival.

The Library Suite retains the true aristocratic flavor of an Italian Renaissance Villa. The living room still has the original wood bookcases on four walls. A carved stone mantel surrounds a fireplace. The dark marble floor is a perfect backdrop for oriental carpets and cherry furniture.

Geneva on the Lake's "Lancellotti Dining Room" offers candlelight gourmet dining on Friday, Saturday and Sunday evenings in magnificent European grandeur. Musical entertainment includes piano, violin, or a vocalist. Breakfast is served daily. Complete dining services for groups are offered daily.

Tasting the master chef's culinary delights, such as mesquite grilled Tournedos a la Bearnaise, Veal Scampi Dianne, or Chicken Jacqueline is an important part of any vacation at Geneva on the Lake. Several culinary weekends, holiday celebrations and mystery weekends are among the special events hosted at the resort.

Owner Norbert Schickel describes the resort as "a little island of beauty, peace and friendliness in a busy world". It is

an ideal setting for the small executive retreat, conference or incentive trip.

Geneva on the Lake is a focal base for exploring the scenic Finger Lakes and nearby attractions including The Corning Glass Center, Sonnenberg Gardens, and 30 local wineries.

OPEN:	Year round
GUEST ROOMS:	29 guest suites, all with ready kitchen. 10 suites have two bedrooms.
RESTAURANT:	Complete breakfast menu daily. Candlelight Gourmet Dining with entertainment on Friday, Saturday and Sunday evenings. Complete cocktail and food service for conferences and groups.
CREDIT CARDS:	Visa, MasterCard, Discover, American Express
RECREATION:	On premises: swimming, sailing, canoeing, fishing, badminton, golf and tennis.
RESTRICTIONS:	Pets
EXTRAS:	Conference suites for up to 40 attendees. Special event weekends planned - holidays, mystery, culinary, etc.

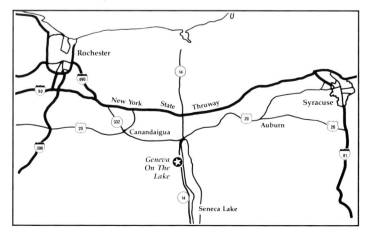

RATES: Seasonal. $110-$271 per room. Includes continental breakfast. (Tax 7%)

DIRECTIONS:
From Interstate 90, the New York State Thruway, take Exit 42 and go south on State Route 14 seven miles to Geneva. The inn is one mile south of Geneva's downtown on Route 14S.

**GENEVA
NEW YORK**

GREGORY HOUSE

Route 43, Averill Park, New York 12018
(518) 674-3774

Around the turn of the century, the many natural lakes and softly rolling hills of the Sand Lake, Averill Park area of upstate New York provided a perfect setting for the popular resort area it would become. Elegant small hotels with Victorian appointed dining rooms catered to the days' carriage trade. A well kept golf course and an old fashioned amusement park with its carousel appealed to young and old alike. A lively night life with New York City entertainers flourished along with the entire area.

The village is quieter now. The lakes and rolling hills are still as beautiful as ever. The golf course is still there, but the area has settled into a peaceful, tranquil suburb of Albany and Troy.

In the midst of this tranquility, you will find the 1840 built home of Elias Gregory, transformed into an unpreten-tious but comfortable country inn. Guests here now enjoy both the serenity of the country and the myriad activities of the surrounding cities. Mountain ranges, lakes, historic sites, and academic facilities are all within an easy drive. Rensselaer Polytechnic Institute, Emma Willard, and Russell Sage educational facilities visitors are frequent guests as are devotees of the Saratoga Performing Arts Center and flat track racing in nearby Saratoga. Tanglewood in the Berkshires, and the downhill slopes at Jiminy Peak and Brodie Mountains, are close by too.

The Gregory House carries on the long tradition of welcoming guests to this beautiful and exciting section of the country. Comfortable rooms, hearty steaks and succulent wines, summer pool and winter fireplaces -- tradition maintained, enhanced.

OPEN:	Year round
GUEST ROOMS:	12 guest rooms, all with private baths, air conditioning and radios.
RESTAURANT:	Continental breakfast served. No lunch served. Dinner served except on Mondays and Christmas Day.
CREDIT CARDS:	American Express, Carte Blanche, Diners Club, MasterCard, Visa
RECREATION:	On premises: Outdoor pool. Nearby: Cross country skiing, fishing, lake, tennis, antiquing, art museums, theatre and historical sights.
RESTRICTIONS:	No children under 6, no pets
EXTRAS:	Meeting space, TV and fireplace in common room.
RATES:	$50-$60 per room. Includes continental breakfast. (Tax 7%)

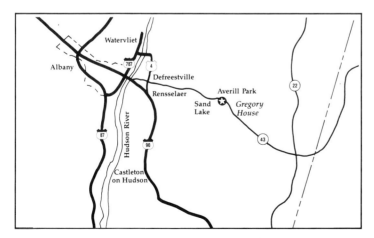

DIRECTIONS:
From I-90 take Exit 7, the first exit East of the Hudson River, and turn left onto Washington Avenue. Continue on Washington across US 4 and take State Route 43 seven and one half miles to Averill Park. Gregory House is on the left.

**AVERILL PARK
NEW YORK**

THE POINT

Star Point, Saranac Lake, New York 12983

(518) 891-5674

For over 100 years the Adirondacks have drawn visitors with their rugged scenery and wilderness beauty. Among the oldest mountain ranges in the world, they abound with unspoiled lakes and trout streams, spectacular gorges and waterfalls, countless miles of hiking trails, and vast, deep forests.

The late nineteenth century was the era of the "Great Camps", which were built by the very wealthy to provide "sumptuous rusticity" for themselves and their friends. One of the finest in this colorful, luxurious tradition is The Point. Designed for William Rockefeller by architect William Distin, it is situated on a secluded peninsula on beautiful Upper Saranac Lake.

Today, visitors to the area can enjoy a myriad of year-round attractions - the Olympic facilities at Lake Placid, spectacular fall foliage displays, and winter festivals.

Only at The Point, can one experience the gracious romantic, and leisurely pace of that bygone era - breakfast in bed, lunch under the hemlocks, cocktail cruises to watch the setting summer sun, followed by candlelit dinner parties where black tie is the suggested (but optional) attire on Wednesday and Saturday evenings. One can find solitude or lively conversation, stimulating exercise or relaxing indolence.

Each of the guest rooms has an individual decor, lake views, spacious private baths, and an eclectic mixture of antiques and Adirondack furniture. Most have king-sized beds, fireplaces of chisled stone and large, walk in closets.

They range in size and style from the snug and cozy Algonquin, with its library-like atmosphere, to the Boathouse, which contains a huge canopied bed, large fireplace, sitting and dining areas, small kitchen, fully stocked bar, and a roofed balcony wrapping all three lake sides of the room.

In the Great Hall gigantic fireplaces blaze at either end with its deep couches, antiques, and moose and deer heads creating an atmosphere of both wilderness elegance and great comfort. It is a fitting setting for elegant dinner parties where the exceptional food and wine is matched by the sparkling company and conversation. The richly varied cuisine, features regional specialties and the freshest of local produce.

OPEN:	Year round
GUEST ROOMS:	11 guest rooms, all with private baths and sitting area. Some of the rooms have fireplaces and terraces.
RESTAURANT:	Breakfast, lunch and dinner served. Cocktails available.
CREDIT CARDS:	American Express
RECREATION:	On premises: boating/canoeing, cross-country skiing, water skiing, fishing, hiking, ice skating, hunting guides, sailing.
RESTRICTIONS:	No handicapped facilities, no children
EXTRAS:	Meeting space, well behaved pets allowed. Children under 18 usually not suitable.
RATES:	$350-$550 per couple per day. Includes meals, activities, and use of recreational equipment. (Tax 7%)

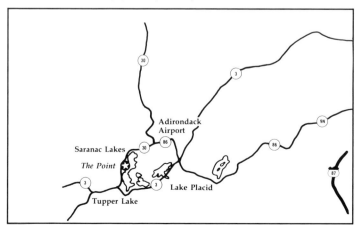

DIRECTIONS:
From I-87, take State Routes 9N and 87 to the town of Saranac Lake. Follow State Route 3 west fifteen miles to the intersection with State Route 30. Go north on State Route 30 six miles to the inn entrace, on the right.

**SARANAC LAKE
NEW YORK**

ROSE INN

813 Auburn Road, Box 6576, Ithaca, New York 14851-6576

(607) 533-4202

This inn is both gracious and romantic. Built in 1850, the two-story Italianate mansion contains some of the most beautiful woodwork and cabinetry you will ever see. Its central focus is a fabulous, wide circular staircase of Honduran mahogany that swirls upwards three stories to the cupola.

The Rose Inn is situated in a magnificent rural setting, in the heart of New York State's Finger Lakes, just minutes from wineries, Cornell University, lake sports, and skiing. Guests can enjoy 20 beautiful acres of lawns and trees -- blue spruce, white birch, sugar maples, and others including a lovely apple orchard.

Inside, the inn displays the ambience of its period. High ceilings, the warm glow of woods from indigenous American trees long gone, marble fireplaces, and period antiques provide an elegant yet comfortable and relaxed setting.

Guests enter the inn through its warm and busy country kitchen into the formal sitting rooms equipped with fireplace, library, games, television, and good conversation.

The guest rooms are spring bright in color, individually and lovingly furnished with great attention to detail for guest needs and comfort. Several suites are available, complete with jacuzzi for two. All rooms have beautiful views of the grounds and pastoral setting.

A full country breakfast is served with apple cider from the inn's own orchard. Also featured are the inn's homemade jams, jellies and apple butter with piping hot croissants.

Guests of the inn are invited to make

reservations for formal dining in the evening. Private dining rooms, candlelight, and sterling silver set the mood. Prix fixe four course meals offer a changing selection of appetizers, entrees, and desserts such as Smoked Oysters in Beurre Blanc on Puff Pastry, Artichoke Heart Strudel, Grilled Whole Norwegian Salmon with Smoked Salmon Mousse and Kiwi, Rack of Lamb with fine herbs, and specialty dessert souffles of pumpkin, apricot or chestnut.

Accompanying dinner is a selective yet comprehensive wine list. The design of the wine list and the dinner selections are unique, and demonstrate chef-owner Sherry Rosemann's commitment to do a "few things perfectly".

OPEN:	Year round
GUEST ROOMS:	17 guest rooms and suites, all with private baths, radios, and phones.
RESTAURANT:	Full breakfast served. Dinner is available Prix Fixe with advance reservations. Closed Mondays and December through March. Wine and beer only.
CREDIT CARDS:	American Express, MasterCard, Visa, Diners Club (see restrictions)
RECREATION:	Nearby: Boating, fishing, antiquing and historical sights.
RESTRICTIONS:	No pets. Deposit must be made by check, final payment by credit card permitted.
EXTRAS:	Meeting space, babysitter
RATES:	$90-$175 per room. Full breakfast included. (Tax 9%)

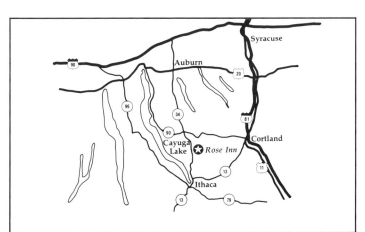

DIRECTIONS:
From North: New York State thruway, Exit 41 (Waterloo), right at 414S, 3/10 of mile to 318E, turn left, for 4.2 miles to 5/20E, left, go 2.1 miles to NY90, right, go 28.8 miles to NY 34S, turn right, go 6.9 miles, the inn is on the left. From South: I-81 to NY79 which goes directly into Ithaca, turn right on Aurora, right on Lincoln, left on Lake, continue on Lake onto Route 34N 9 miles, inn is on right.

ITHACA
NEW YORK

TROUTBECK

Leedsville Road, Amenia, New York 12501

(914) 373-9681

Troutbeck is an English Country Estate with a literate and liberal history. While only two hours from midtown Manhattan, Troutbeck is far from the urgencies of today's world. The handsome grounds are bordered by a bubbling brook, a wandering river, and towering trees (a row of 200 foot high sycamores planted in 1835 provide a frontispiece for the house). The inn also offers a covered, heated indoor swimming pool with sauna and exercise room, a large outdoor pool, two tennis courts, volleyball, jogging trails, and a

small lake and stream for fishing.

Many of the bedrooms in the main house have canopy beds, fireplaces and porches. In the "Century," the 18th century American farmhouse, there are additional bedrooms, some with fireplaces, and canopy beds. The Century is only 225 footsteps away from the main house.

Besides the fine food and a beautiful home and grounds, there are also movies on videotape, 12,000 books, a wonderful poker table, and surrounding attractions in the foothills of the Berkshires --summer theatre, antiquing, historic homes, and beautiful New England villages. There are also golf courses, riding stables, Limerock Racetrack, and nearby vineyards.

Highly respected in the corporate world as an executive retreat, Troutbeck functions as a country inn only on weekends. Guests arrive at 5 p.m. Friday, and stay until Sunday at 2 p.m. The weekend rates include all meals and all spirits, even wine. For corporate groups, the conference room, like the rest of the house, is beamed and fireplaced. During the gentle months, both conferees and weekenders are invited out to have lunch beside the outdoor pool -- everyone's favorite meal.

Once written of Troutbeck, "Troutbeck still offers a link between a family and a landscape, between a patch of historic soil and the generations that are still to come. No feudal continuity of blood, but a democratic continuity of spirit binds together the families that have occupied Troutbeck...a pattern of life and a gentle breed of men and women; people like Wordsworth's Lucy, who "dwell in beauty" and unconsciously carry some of that beauty into their daily actions. This quality is beyond any price...but whoever learns to love Troutbeck will find that it is the most precious part of the bargain."

OPEN:	Year round
GUEST ROOMS:	31 guest rooms and suites, most with private baths. 24 hour phone service available. Some rooms with fireplaces and porches.
RESTAURANT:	Breakfast, lunch and dinner served.
CREDIT CARDS:	American Express
RECREATION:	On premises: indoor pool, sauna and exercise room, outdoor pool, tennis courts, volleyball, jogging trails, small lake and stream for fishing.
RESTRICTIONS:	No children between 1 and 12, open to public on weekends only.
EXTRAS:	Snacks and spirits. Babysitter, cribs available. Conference center.
RATES:	$550-$775 per couple for weekend stay. All meals included. Call for conference group rates. (Tax 3%)

DIRECTIONS:
Route 684 North to Brewster. Stay on 684 (six lanes) Don't turn. Past Brewster 684 becomes Route 22. Turn right at the light onto Route 343 heading for Sharon, CT. Go 2.4 miles. You'll see our sign on your right, turn right beyond the sign onto a paved road, cross a river/bridge in about 50 yeards and Troutbeck is the first driveway on your right.

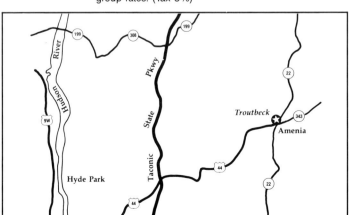

**AMENIA
NEW YORK**

WHITE INN

52 East Main Street, Scenic Route 20, Fredonia, New York 14063
(716) 672-2103

Historic Fredonia is just 3 miles from Lake Erie in far-western New York State. It is a town with many nineteenth-century buildings surrounding a double common complete with an iron fountain and a Victorian bandstand, where summer concerts are performed. This town is home to Fredonia State University College, offering cultural and sporting events year round.

The postcard perfect White Inn has a 100-foot long veranda shaded by ancient maple trees planted by the original owner, Dr. Squire White, back in 1821. It was one of the charter members of the Duncan Hines Family of Fine Restaurants.

The recently restored inn has built its considerable reputation on a combination of unique features. The inn has an international reputation for exquisite meals at very reasonable prices and also has beautifully restored rooms, antique furnishings, several suites, designer wallpapers, and antiques for sale in the public areas.

Lake Chautauqua, forty minutes away, is the home of the Chautauqua Institute. This world famous cultural and religious center is renowned for the speakers and musical soloists who appear every summer.

Flower gardens adorn the property and the kitchen herbs are fresh from the inn's own garden.

In addition, the inn has a gorgeous 37 foot sailboat, which frequently sails the waters of nearby Lake Erie with guests from the inn. Another attraction is a tandem bicycle available to tour the Victorian village. Nearby are several wineries

whose excellent vintages may be sampled free of charge. Dozens of antique stores are within a 20 minute drive.

Lake Erie, with its boating, swimming and water skiing is only minutes away.

Guests are served a complimentary Continental breakfast. The dining rooms are open to the public for daily breakfast, lunch and dinner. The menu offers fresh local produce and meats along with soups, breads and desserts created from scratch.

OPEN:	Year round
GUEST ROOMS:	20 guest rooms and suites, all with private baths, phones and TVs.
RESTAURANT:	3 dining rooms serving breakfast, lunch and dinner daily. Lounge.
CREDIT CARDS:	American Express, MasterCard, Visa
RECREATION:	On premises: bicycles. Nearby: boating, crosscountry and downhill skiing, fishing, golf, jogging, picnic area, lake, indoor and outdoor pool and antiquing.
RESTRICTIONS:	No pets, no handicap facilities
EXTRAS:	Elevator, meeting space
RATES:	$39-$69 per room. Continental breakfast included. (Tax 7%)

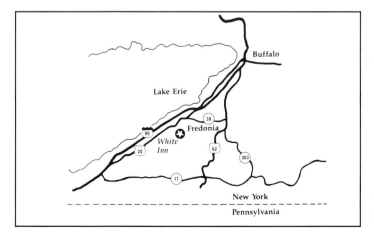

DIRECTIONS:
The inn is in downtown Fredonia on U.S. 20 (Main Street), southwest of Buffalo.

**FREDONIA
NEW YORK**

BROOKSTOWN INN

200 Brookstown Avenue, Winston-Salem, North Carolina 27101

(919) 725-1120

In 1766, a group of Moravians -- devout Germanic people who had first settled this section of North Carolina in 1753 -- founded a small congregation town. They called it "Salem" from the Hebrew word for "peace", an appropriate name for those who were later called "the quiet people of the land." As planned, Salem became a commercial center not only for the Moravians living in the area but also for settlers of the entire region. People came from miles around to buy the wares of the skilled Moravian craftsmen. By 1836, the Moravian governing boards authorized the establishment of a "modern" cotton mill in Salem.

Today, the Brookstown Mill complex has been adapted to new uses, including the Brookstown Inn. From the mo-

ment you enter the lobby you will know that this is an extraordinary hostelry. The Brookstown Inn is a caring restoration of an historically important landmark.

Each room is different, due to the intent of the owners to incorporate modern lodging comforts and preserve significant achitectural features. The furnishings were chosen to capture the charm of our Early American heritage.

The public areas of the inn are equally unique. The Parlor, a large sitting room/library, has several areas for reading, games or business discussions. Each evening, guests are offered a selection of domestic wines and cheeses here to get the evening off to a good start.

In the dining room, adjacent to The Parlor, a light breakfast is served each morning. Included are the famous Moravian pastries from nearby Old Salem.

The Brookstown Inn is delightfully convenient to the Winston-Salem commercial district. For those more interested in history, the inn sits on the boundary of Old Salem, the restored Moravian town. Most sunny afternoons a horse drawn carriage is ready to take you to Old Salem, in 19th century style.

OPEN:	Year round
GUEST ROOMS:	52 guest rooms and suites, all with private baths, phones, TVs, and radios. Some with whirlpool baths.
RESTAURANT:	Light breakfast served. Restaurant and lounge adjacent.
CREDIT CARDS:	American Express, MasterCard, Visa
RECREATION:	On premises: library, jogging, bicycling. Nearby: picnic area, golf, art museums, crafts, historical sights, theatre.
RESTRICTIONS:	No pets
EXTRAS:	Elevator, valet, babysitter
RATES:	$65-$85 per room. Light breakfast and wine and cheese included. (Tax 8%)

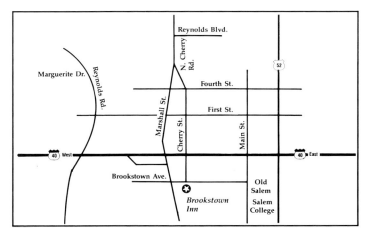

DIRECTIONS:
Leave I-40 at Cherry Street exit in downtown Winston-Salem. Go South on Marshall Street, parallel to Cherry. About one half mile turn left onto Brookstown Avenue. The first building in the Mill Complex is the inn.

**WINSTON-SALEM
NORTH CAROLINA**

FEARRINGTON HOUSE

The Fearrington Village Center, Pittsboro, North Carolina 27312
(919) 542-4000, (800) 334-5475

etween Chapel Hill and Pittsboro, you will discover the historic Fearrington Farm. Throughout its long history, this 625 acre farm has changed. During the 1780's it was a cotton and tobacco farm, with a magnificent farmhouse built in 1829. The farm flourished until the Civil War and the fall of King Cotton in the 1860's. In 1925 the original house burned and a new one was built and in the 1930's Fearrington Farm became a dairy farm.

In 1974, Jesse Fearrington sold the farm. Although the new owners were no longer interested in farming, they were interested in preserving the farm itself. Not as a museum but as living proof of the durability of its character.

Today the original homeplace is a restaurant of fine cuisine serving dinner and Sunday brunch. Articles in many major magazines attest to its excellence. A constantly changing menu features local fish, fowl and produce, from coastal red snapper to Carolina quail smoked over applewood. Also, the Fearrington House Restaurant offers guests a wide

collection of wines primarily from small, select California vineyards.

The Village of Fearrington includes the Market, a gourmet deli, bakery, and grocery in the old grainery. Next door a converted milk barn houses a pottery shop, needlepoint and jewelery shops, and a Southern garden shop set amidst beautiful vistas complete with bluebirds, hollyhocks and Belted Galloway cows.

Inspiration to add overnight accommodations came from the owners delightful experiences in the country inns of England and France. In November of 1986 the inn was opened to guests. Although relatively new, the architecture blends with the original homeplace so well the feeling of history surrounds you. All of the rooms and suites are individually designed to capture distinctive moods. You will find comfort and charm created by a blend of antiques, original art, and tasteful appointments.

OPEN:	Year round
GUEST ROOMS:	14 guest rooms and suites, all private baths, phones, TVs and radios.
RESTAURANT:	Dinner served nightly except Sunday, Monday, Christmas and New Years Day. Beer and wine available in the pub.
CREDIT CARDS:	MasterCard, Visa
RECREATION:	On premises: Bicycles, fishing, hot tub, jacuzzi, jogging, picnic areas, outdoor pool. Nearby: Boating, lake,racquetball, antiquing.
RESTRICTIONS:	No children under 12, no pets (kennels nearby). No smoking in guest or dining rooms.
EXTRAS:	Handicapped facilities, meeting space

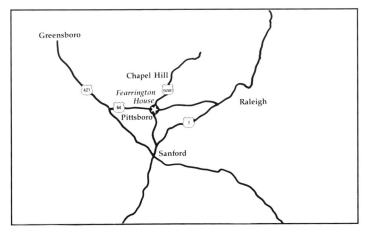

RATES:
$75-$175 per room. Includes continental breakfast. Complimentary fruit and cheese on arrival. (Tax 5%)

DIRECTIONS:
Off I-85 to 15-501 south through Chapel Hill. 8 miles outside Chapel Hill on 15-501.

**CHAPEL HILL
NORTH CAROLINA**

HARMONY HOUSE INN

215 Pollock Street, New Bern, North Carolina 28560

(919) 636-3810

New Bern, North Carolina, known by the Indians as Chattawka or "where the fish are taken out" was founded in 1710 by the Swiss and Germans at the confluence of the Neuse and Trent rivers. Its prosperity and strategic location made it the site for Royal Governor Tryon's Palace and the seat of government in 1770. It later became the government center for the state of North Carolina.

Harmony House Inn is in New Bern's Historic District which contains outstanding examples of American architecture from colonial days to the early 20th century. Many of these homes are open to the public during the Spring Old Homes Tour and the Fall New Bern at Night. The magnificent Palace gardens are open free during some of the town's festivities such as the Chrysanthemum Festival in October and the Spring and

Fall Colonial Living Days. Harmony House is designated an Historic Point of Interest and is near Tryon Palace, shops, and restaurants.

Benjamin Ellis, the grandson of an early New Bern settler, built the first four rooms of the inn around 1850. As his family grew to six children, he added four rooms about 1860 and four more around 1880. In 1900, the house was sawed in half, the west side moved over nine feet, and a second hallway, front door, staircase, and four more rooms were added. The large rooms and double hallway make this an unusually spacious country inn.

Comfortable elegance is apparent from the antique and reproduction (many locally made) furnishings. The guest rooms have either one queen bed or two twin beds, two comfortable chairs (for watching cable TV), air-conditioning, ceiling fans and even electric blankets for our few cold nights! Guests will find an assortment of magazines and books. A refrigerator with complimentary soft drinks and juices is available to enjoy in the parlor, in rocking chairs on the front porch, or in the beautifully landscaped backyard. The dining room has an Empire buffet where a full homemade breakfast is served including a freshly ground coffee blended especially for us.

OPEN:	Year round
GUEST ROOMS:	9 guest rooms, all private baths and TVs. Phones available.
RESTAURANT:	Buffet breakfast served. Restaurants within walking distance for lunch and dinner.
CREDIT CARDS:	American Express, MasterCard, Visa
RECREATION:	Nearby: Bicycling, boating, fishing, jogging, walking paths, picnic areas, sailing, tennis, theatre.
RESTRICTIONS:	No pets
RATES:	$50-$65 per room. Includes buffet breakfast. (Tax 8%)

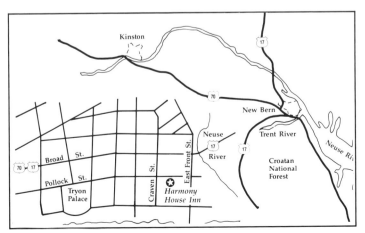

DIRECTIONS:
From US 17 in New Bern, go south on Craven Street one block, then turn left onto Pollock Street. The inn is on the right.

NEW BERN
NORTH CAROLINA

THE HOLLY INN

Cherokee Road, Box 2300, Pinehurst, North Carolina 28374
(919) 295-2300, (800) 682-6901 (inside North Carolina),
(800) 533-0041 (out of state)

Amidst the majestic long-leaf pines and colorful sandhills of North Carolina, this charming five-story country inn is located in the historic village of Pinehurst, one of America's premier golf resorts.

In addition to over 30 golf courses, designed by the likes of Donald Ross,

Jack Nicklaus and Reese Jones, guests of the Holly Inn can enjoy other sports facilities including horseback riding, bicycling, and tennis. Water activities are available on a 200 acre lake. Guests enjoy sport and skeet shooting at the same gun club where Annie Oakley taught in 1915.

Touring turn of the century houses, strolling through the picture-postcard New England Style village which still maintains the look much as it did at the turn of the century with its shops, boutiques and sun-warmed verandas, and visiting the World Golf Hall of Fame are favorite activities.

The Holly Inn was built in 1895 in the center of 5,890 acres of wasteland purchased by James Walker Tufts. Tufts commissioned Frederick Law Olmstead, famed landscape architect who designed New York's Central Park, to draw a set of plans for a village with open park spaces and winding streets. A most impressive volume of construction was undertaken including iron rails for a trolley to operate up and down Main Street. In those early days, before a power plant was built or electric lines were strung, the trolley was drawn by horses.

The Holly's first brochure boasted of electric lights, steam heat, telephones, a solarium, billiard room, an orchestra and an abundance of choice foods.

For over 90 years the Holly Inn has remained the crown jewel of Pinehurst. Today, listed on the National Register of Historic Buildings and Sites, the Holly Inn offers 77 guest rooms, 33 of which are suites, each having its own special style and distinctive characteristics. In one, a shadowy alcove invites intimate conversation. In another, a sloping roof line forms a cozy corner.

Dining may be enjoyed in the newly renovated octagon-shaped dining room with its peaked roof, fireplace, and light walls with floor-to-ceiling windows. The Chef is quickly adding to his already renowned reputation, with innovative and appealing menus. A special blend of Southern Regional Cuisine is served daily for breakfast, lunch and dinner.

OPEN:	Year round
GUEST ROOMS:	77 guest rooms and suites, all with private baths, phones, TVs, radios and work areas. Some suites with wet bars and fireplaces.
RESTAURANT:	Breakfast, lunch and dinner served daily. Lounge with entertainment.
CREDIT CARDS:	American Express, MasterCard, Diners Club, Visa, Carte Blanche
RECREATION:	On premises: Outdoor pool, historical sights. Nearby: Lake, boating, fishing, golf, hot tubs, jacuzzi, sailing, sauna and racquetball.
RESTRICTIONS:	No pets
EXTRAS:	Elevator, valet, babysitting, meeting space
RATES:	$85-$120 per room. Full breakfast included for $5 per person additional. (Tax 5%)

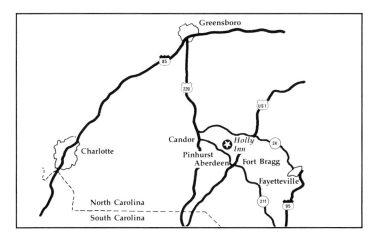

DIRECTIONS:
Route 95 to Route 211 to Pinehurst Circle, Hall of Fame exit, right on Fields then left onto Cherokee

PINEHURST
NORTH CAROLINA

MEADOWBROOK INN

Main Street, Blowing Rock, North Carolina 28605
(704) 295-9341, (800) 456-5456

Meadowbrook Inn is the perfect mountain retreat, nestled among lovely gardens alongside a cool bubbly stream. Although recently built, Meadowbrook Inn can best be described as a European Country Hotel, providing the intimate qualities of a small inn, with many of the services expected in a world-class hotel.

The spacious guest rooms and suites are furnished with imported floral

fabrics and traditional reproduction period furniture. The surroundings exude an air of casual elegance.

Breakfast, lunch and dinner are all special occasions served in the Garden Restaurant. Overlooking the lovely gardens, lush with native shrubbery and flowers, the Garden Restaurant features distinctive American cuisine and fine wines. The everchanging menu assures the freshest of the season.

The Garden Lounge is the perfect spot to gather with friends, old and new. The ambience is casual and comfortable, allowing you to relax and enjoy your favorite cocktail. Perhaps you have a request for the pianist.

While staying at the Meadowbrook Inn, day trips to Boone, Beech Mountain and Banner Elk should be on your itinerary. Area attractions include Grandfather Mountain, Daniel Boone Native Gardens, Linville Caverns, Mystery Hill, Tweetsie Railroad and "Horn in the West" outdoor drama.

Blowing Rock is surrounded by mountains that some geologists have judged to be among the oldest rock formations in the world. Bishop August Spangenberg explored this region in 1752 in search of land for Moravian colonists and Daniel Boone hunted here in the 1760s. The Cherokees once claimed this area as a hunting ground. Finally in 1800, the county was inhabited by immigrants from Pennsylvania, New Jersey and New England. The current inhabitants welcome you to share their peaceful and history laden area.

OPEN:	Year round
GUEST ROOMS:	47 guest rooms and suites, all with private baths, phones, TVs. Some with fireplaces and whirlpool baths.
RESTAURANT:	Breakfast, lunch and dinner served daily except Mondays Nov. 1 - May 31. Lounge.
CREDIT CARDS:	American Express, Visa, MasterCard
RECREATION:	Nearby: Boating, cross-country and downhill skiing, fishing, golf, jogging, walking paths, pools, tennis, antiquing and crafts.
RESTRICTIONS:	No pets
EXTRAS:	Elevator, babysitting, meeting space.
RATES:	$56-$180 per room. Continental breakfast included. (Tax 8%)

DIRECTIONS:
From I40 to 321, also known as Main Street, to Blowing Rock.

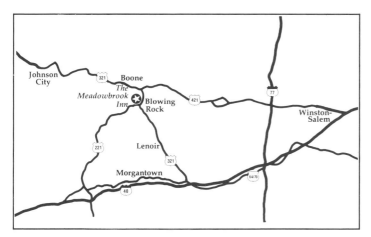

BLOWING ROCK
NORTH CAROLINA

SANDERLING INN

SR Box 319Y DUCK, Kitty Hawk, North Carolina 27949

(919) 261-4111

The natural beauty and architectural heritage of North Carolina's Outer Banks flourish in the serenity of a fine inn called Sanderling.

The Sanderling Inn has proudly set the highest standards in architecture and conservation to be found on the Outer Banks. With the Atlantic Ocean to the east, the Currituck Sound to the west and the Pine Island National Audubon Sanctuary to the north -- Sanderling Inn's own natural beauty is buffered from encroachment.

Named for the small waterbird that bears its name, the handsome Sanderling Inn awaits you amidst 3,400 acres of natural coastal beauty. Designed and furnished in the grande tradition of a bygone era, this gracious inn offers its guests comforts and amenities found in the world's finest hotels. Imported toiletries, plush monogrammed bathrobes, fresh fruit and wine are but a few of the personal touches provided for your comfort. Fully equipped kitchens, private porches with breathtaking views and elegant furnishings appoint each guest's suite. The Grand Gallery and Audubon Room provide a relaxing setting for social gatherings amidst a fine collection of porcelains, paintings, handsome antiques and an extensive library of books and periodicals. Private ocean beach and Currituck Sound frontage offer easy access for water sports and recreation.

Next door to the inn, the restaurant's chefs prepare superb regional cuisine from the freshest ingredients to be

served in a beautifully restored turn of the century U.S. Life Saving Station. The building has been placed on the National Register of Historic Places and contains a fine collection of nautical antiques.

The Sanderling Inn was built in the grande tradition of historic inns and famous hotels, and is in harmony with its Outer Banks setting. At the Sanderling Inn guests are treated to Carolina hospitality at its best.

OPEN:	Year round
GUEST ROOMS:	28 rooms including loft suites, all with private baths, phones, TVs and radios.
RESTAURANT:	Breakfast, lunch, and dinner served Memorial Day through Labor Day. Limited off season service for inn guests. Catering and room service available.
CREDIT CARDS:	American Express, MasterCard, Visa
RECREATION:	On premises: Boat dock and ramp, outdoor pool, tennis courts. Nearby: ocean, fishing, theatre, sailing, golf, historical sights, and seasonal festivals.
RESTRICTIONS:	No pets
EXTRAS:	Meeting space
RATES:	$65-$200 double occupancy. Continental breakfast included during summer months. (Tax 8%)

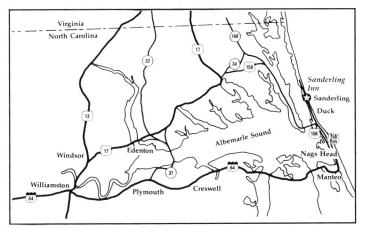

DIRECTIONS:
From Elizabeth City, take US 158 east and south to Kitty Hawk. Turn left at the first traffic light past the Duck Woods Golf Club, and follow the main road north through Duck to the Sanderling Inn.

KITTY HAWK
NORTH CAROLINA

WOOSTER INN

East Wayne Avenue at Gasche Street, Wooster, Ohio 44691

(216) 264-2341

Adjoining The College of Wooster Golf Course and overlooking the rolling country side of Ohio, The Wooster Inn is located in this small and thriving college town in the Midwestern Heartland between Columbus and Cleveland, Akron and Mansfield. To the south is the largest Amish settlement in the state and Mohican State Park.

Wooster was first settled in 1808 by William Henry, John Bevek, and the Larwill Brothers. The town was named after General David Wooster, a revolutionary war hero.

The present day Public Square boasts the ornate Wyane County Courthouse, built in 1878. Most of the Squares commercial buildings date from the Victorian 1880's and 1890's.

Wooster is the home of the Ohio Light Opera where, in the summer months, Gilbert and Sullivan and other well-known operettas are performed. In the fall, the area is known for its beautiful fall foliage. Visitors from far away make Wooster their headquarters from which to soak in beauty before the beginning of the winter season. While guests may enjoy golf in the warmer months, during winter the golf course is perfect for cross-country skiing. In the spring, the nearby Ohio Agriculture Research and Development Station's extensive crabapple alleys attract a great many nature lovers. Later, it is azalea and rose garden time.

From the beginning, Wooster, the county seat of Wayne County, has been a staging post for the movement West, and besides agriculture, oil drilling,

banking and stores, there was little commerce. The town now offers guests all the activities of a vibrant college town.

The College of Wooster was founded in 1866 and excels in liberal arts and music. Since there was always a need to house visitors and visiting dignitaries, The Wooster Inn was conceived, and under the leadership of, and with donations by Mr. Robert E. Wilson in honor of his parents, the inn was opened to the public in 1959. The inn is now the county's foremost hostelry.

The seventeen tastefully decorated guest rooms are maintained to offer modern comfort and quiet.

Dinner at The Wooster Inn is a relaxing and elegant occassion. The menu includes Fillet of Fresh Rainbow Trout, Veal Scaloppine al Marsala, Steak al Poivre, Sherried Breast of Chicken, Shrimp Scampi, fresh pasta, homemade soups and desserts. Aperitifs and select wines are served with dinners. Intimate dinners and business meetings can be arranged. House guests enjoy a full complimentary breakfast.

OPEN: Year round

GUEST ROOMS: 17 guest rooms and suites, all with private baths, phones and TVs.

RESTAURANT: Breakfast, lunch and dinner served daily except Christmas day.

CREDIT CARDS: American Express, MasterCard, Visa, Diners Club

RECREATION: On premises: cross-country skiing, golf, walking path. Nearby: Jogging, racquet-ball, indoor pool, tennis and antiquing.

RESTRICTIONS: Small pets only

EXTRAS: Elevator, babysitting, meeting space

RATES: $42-$120 per room. Breakfast included. (Tax 8.5%)

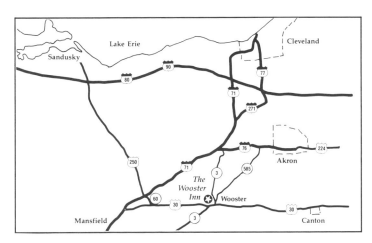

DIRECTIONS:
From US 250 bypass, exit at State Route 585 and go south to Wayne Avenue. Turn right and continue around golf course to the inn.

**WOOSTER
OHIO**

WORTHINGTON INN

649 High Street, Worthington, Ohio 43085
(614) 885-2600

The second oldest continuously operating inn in Ohio, the Worthington Inn was built as a stagecoach stop in 1831, and has been in business ever since. The architecture is a pleasant combination of all the eras in which the inn has served, including Federal, Greek Revival and Victorian.

Each of the guest suites is individually appointed with Sheraton, Hepplewhite or Victorian pieces. Some chambers have been meticulously hand-stenciled for an Early American look. Others feature rich turn-of-the-century textiles and fixtures.

Each of the three restored dining rooms on the main floor reflect the hand-crafted artifacts of bygone eras. A strong regional american influence dictates the highly acclaimed menu featuring seafood, veal, beef and fowl specialties. From the inn's bakery, the rich aromas of irresistable delicacies beckon you to sample and enjoy.

An extensive wine collection is held in a cellar tightly sealed with an authentic hand-wrought dungeon door to insure proper storage.

The Pub Room invites guests to relax with a favorite beverage, and perhaps a hearty sandwich in it's Victorian elegance including the long, marble-topped bar.

Nearby to Worthington are the Campuses of Ohio State University, Otterbein University, and Ohio Wesleyan University with an array of cultural and athletic events throughout the year. Guests may play golf at the Indian Hills Country Club.

All of the attractions of Columbus, a bright, energetic and growing city await you only minutes away.

OPEN:	Year round
GUEST ROOMS:	24 rooms and suites, all with private baths, phones and TVs.
RESTAURANT:	Continental breakfast with champagne. Lunch, dinner and weekend brunch served daily. Lounge serves light fare.
CREDIT CARDS:	American Express, Diners Club, MasterCard, Visa, Discover
RECREATION:	Library, historical sights, antiquing and jogging. University campus activities, theater, musical performances.
RESTRICTIONS:	No pets (kennel available).
EXTRAS:	Turndown service, complimentary champagne, meeting space, valet, babysitting, handicap facilities, meeting space, limousine service available.

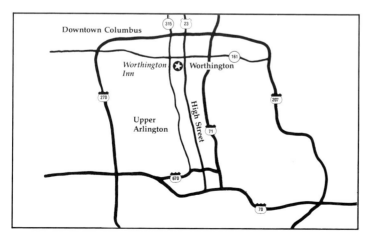

RATES:
$95-$125 per room, double occupancy. Continental breakfast included. (Tax 5.5%)

DIRECTIONS:
From I71, take Exit 117, State Route 161, west two miles to State Route 23, High Street. The inn is on High Street between 161 and New England Avenue.

WORTHINGTON OHIO

CAMERON ESTATE INN

RD #1, Box 305, Mount Joy, Pennsylvania 17552

(717) 653-1773

Nestled deep in the countryside of Northwestern Lancaster County, historic Cameron Estate Inn is nearly hidden from view by huge old trees gracing the fifteen acres. Stocked trout streams, trails through the wooded areas, books and games by the library fireplace, antiques and candlelight dining make each guest feel like they have stepped back in time.

The farmlands surrounding the inn change with each season. New fallen snow creates a winter wonderland just perfect for cross country skiing, skating or sitting by a fireplace. Spring brings wild flowers, tulips, dogwood, flowering trees and shrubs. The fields look like a patchwork quilt of hay, wheat, corn, tobacco, tomatoes and vegetables. The narrow roads are an adventure, even a challenge, as you discover nearby covered bridges, historic Maytown, Mount Joy, Marietta, Columbia and Wrightsville. The wineries, antique shops, biking and hiking trails, sky diving, ballooning, boating, tubing, golf, tennis, swimming and shopping (outlet and specialty) could keep one busy for weeks.

Lancaster County's farmer's markets and perfectly manicured vegetable and flower gardens are a rare treat for the camera buff. The huge porches surrounding the inn provide the perfect spot to relax and watch the birds and wildlife, especially the millions of fireflies that light up the night skies from late June 'til September. Next to the inn you can enjoy a walk and visit to the historic Donegal Church, founded before 1722 and famous for the Revolutionary War tradition of the Witness Tree.

Harvest time, fall foliage, football games, house tours, candlelight tours, holiday house tours, walking tours, museums, art shows and galleries, festivals, community farm fairs, fire company suppers, church suppers and auctions provide weekly entertainment. There are quarterly schedules of all planned festivals and activities available upon request from the Pennsylvania Dutch Visitors Bureau.

Listed on the National Register of Historic Places, equal distance from Lancaster, Hershey and York, Cameron Estate Inn celebrates the elegant lifestyle of Simon Cameron and family, the famous politician known as "The Cameron Machine". Each of the eighteen rooms have been thoughtfully restored with antiques and period reproductions. The seven rooms with fireplaces, oriental rugs, quilts and wing chairs for relaxing and reading are as large as most living rooms. Most have private baths and the dormer rooms are so cozy. All guests are offered continental breakfast and the same turndown service, view and gran-

deur of the "old days". The winding stairways to the third floor leading to the enormous skylight with hanging planters remind one of "Gone with the Wind".

The dining room and enclosed porch feature carefully prepared American and Continental cuisine. The cut crystal globes sparkle as the candlelight dances around the crystal and china table settings. The chefs and friendly staff make each meal a memorable experience, serving thick juicy steaks, veal, duck, chicken and delicate seafood entrees with the freshest of vegetables and a tempting array of desserts. Each lunch, dinner and Sunday champagne brunch also features the chef's "inspiration of the day." An extensive wine list and cocktails are always available.

OPEN:	Year round
GUEST ROOMS:	18 guest rooms, 16 with private baths. Some with four poster beds and working fireplaces.
RESTAURANT:	Continental breakfast served, not available Christmas day; lunch, dinner available except on Sundays & Christmas day.
CREDIT CARDS:	American Express, MasterCard, Visa
RECREATION:	Nearby: bicycling, fishing, games, hiking, boating, golf, sailing, tennis, swimming, hot air balloon rides, downhill skiing, TV in Library.
RESTRICTIONS:	No handicapped facilities, no pets, no children under 12. 2 night minimum on weekends.
EXTRAS:	Meeting space

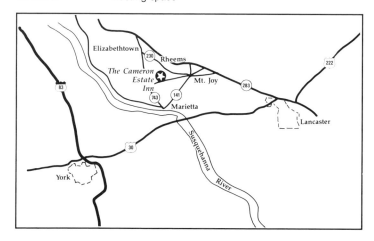

RATES:
$60-$95 per room, includes continental breakfast. (Tax 6%)

DIRECTIONS:
3 miles from Mount Joy, 11 from Lancaster, 12 from Hershey, 25 from Harrisburg or York on Donegal off of Route 743

**MOUNT JOY
PENNSYLVANIA**

EVERMAY-ON-THE-DELAWARE

River Road, Erwinna, Pennsylvania 18920

(215) 294-9100

This significant riverside mansion reflects the prominence of the two Bucks County families with which the property was long associated. Built upon land once owned by Colonel Arthur Erwin, the area's wealthiest gentleman, the residence was enlarged to its present dimensions in 1871. During the late 19th and early 20th century, the house served as a summer hotel and attracted such noted guests as members of the theatrical Barrymore clan.

The manor house and carriage house dominate twenty-five acres of gardens, woodlawn paths and pastures that stretch from the Delaware River to the Delaware Canal. The inn combines the romance and isolation of a historic mansion with the formalities of a small, elegant hotel.

Up the grand staircase are eleven rooms and suites, each named after a notable Bucks County personality and each with private bath and appointed with Victorian antiques. Fresh flowers and fruit are always in the guest rooms

in the main house and in the carriage house.

Dining is a significant part of a guest's stay at Evermay-on-the-Delaware, whether at breakfast, afternoon tea or dinner. Breakfast is served in a conservatory on the first floor of the inn and afternoon tea either outside on the patio or in the Library/Parlor. On Friday,

Saturday, Sunday and holidays, guests sit down to a very special evening meal that begins with hors d'oeuvres and champagne followed by six carefully prepared courses. Your entrees might include Muscove Duck Breast with Lingonberries, Poached Norwegian Salmon with Leeks and Lobster, Roast Loin of Veal with Morels or Loin of Lamb with Green Peppercorns.

Aside from the privacy, beautiful setting and fine dining, you will find no planned activities here. Nevertheless, the location of Evermay-on-the-Delaware places you within minutes of canoeing, sailing on Lake Nockamixon, cross country skiing, shopping in Flemington, New Jersey or New Hope, and all the artistic, historic and scenic beauty that has made Bucks County famous. Bucks County is a year round destination with art and antique shows, recitals and theatre scheduled throughout.

OPEN:	Year round except December 24th.
GUEST ROOMS:	16 guest rooms and suites, all with private baths. TVs and phones available.
RESTAURANT:	Breakfast, afternoon tea available 7 days a week. Dinner on Friday, Saturday, Sunday and holidays only at 7:30pm.
CREDIT CARDS:	MasterCard, Visa
RECREATION:	Nearby: Cross-country skiing, canoeing, sailing, horseback riding, fishing, historic sights, antiquing and theatre.
RESTRICTIONS:	Not appropriate for children and pets, no singles on weekends, minimum stay required on certain holidays.
EXTRAS:	Meeting space
RATES:	$60-$110 per room. Includes Continental breakfast and afternoon tea. (Tax 6%)

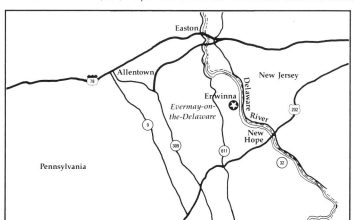

DIRECTIONS:
From North: take NJ Turnpike to Exit I-78 west to Exit 15 (Pittstown NJ) cross bridge to Pennsylvania. Turn left on Route 32 (River Road). Inn is 1.5 miles on right. From South: I-95 to first exit in New Jersey (Route 29N) through Lambertville to Frenchtown.

**ERWINNA
PENNSYLVANIA**

GENERAL SUTTER INN

14 East Main Street, Lititz, Pennsylvania 17543

(717) 626-2115

Located on the square in the quaint 18th century village of Lititz, the historic General Sutter Inn has the enviable distinction of being the oldest continuously operating inn in Pennsylvania. The town itself was founded in 1764. That same year, because town law decreed "no giving a night's lodging to any person," the inn was founded by the Church for "the necessary entertainment of strangers and travellers." Originally called "Zum Anker" the inn has continued for over 220 years its proud tradition of offering gracious hospitality.

The dining room, amidst flickering oil lamps, offers American and Continental cuisine featuring such specialties as Filet Mignon topped with Fresh Crabmeat, Roast Duckling in a Peach Brandy Sauce, fresh seafood and tender veal. Not to be missed are the homemade soup, bread and the scrumptious desserts.

Each guest room of the inn is individually decorated and furnished with Victorian antiques. Oriental style carpets cover newly redone floors. Quilts top elaborate, high-backed country beds and lace curtains grace the windows. Every dresser features 1920 comb and brush sets. "Like Grandma's house" is a comment often heard.

A library is available for guests for quiet conversation, a game of checkers or cards or just to curl-up in a lounge chair and read a good book.

As a guest recently wrote: " Occasionally places are as good as one remembers, but rarely better. The General Sutter is one of those rare, happy exceptions. The rooms are visually beautiful and seductively comfortable. The dining

room is elegant and the food truly cuisine. The birds are charming and the staff exceptional."

Lititz, where chimes mark the passing of time, offers charming shops, America's oldest pretzel bakery and the alluring scent of chocolate from the Wilbur Chocolate Factory. During the summer there are sidewalk antique, craft and art shows. Extra special is the old fashioned Independence Day celebration with thousands of candles lighting the park and a crowning fireworks display. Christmas sees a town festively decorated and a host of people who participate in the Moravian Love Feast.

OPEN:	Year round except Christmas Eve, Christmas Day and January 1
GUEST ROOMS:	12 guest rooms and suites, all private baths, phones, black and white TVs, radios.
RESTAURANT:	Cafe serves breakfast and lunch daily. Formal dining room serves lunch and dinner. Lounge available for fine wine and spirits, also serves lunch and dinner.
CREDIT CARDS:	American Express, Visa, MasterCard
RECREATION:	On Premises: Library, game tables. Nearby: Antiquing, historical sights.
EXTRAS:	Babysitter, meeting space
RATES:	$60-$80 per room. (Tax 6%)

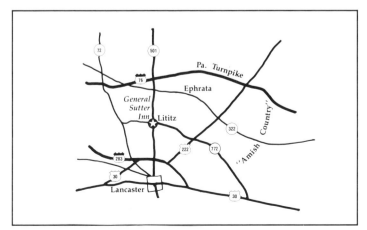

DIRECTIONS:
From south: 501N 6 miles to Lititz. Inn is on 501. From north: Route 78 to 501S, 25 miles to Lititz.

**LITITZ
PENNSYLVANIA**

THE GLASBERN

Pack House Road, Fogelsville, Pennsylvania 18051
(215) 285-4723

A renovated 19th Century bank barn, located on 16 acres of rolling Pennsylvania Dutch farmland just 10 minutes west of Allentown, Glasbern offers luxurious accommodations, some with fireplaces and whirlpools.

The recently renovated Carriage House and outdoor pool are surrounded by hillsides of peach and apple orchards. The majestic Great Room with its exposed hand-hewn beams and interior walls of native stone, is reminiscent of times gone by.

Everything comes alive in the spring with hiking trails and gardens in full bloom. The two ponds on the property have thawed after a long winter and country life awakens.

In summer, enjoy your favorite beverage while sunning next to the new swimming pool, a favorite during the hot months. A hot air balloon ride departing from Glasbern will liven up any lazy summer day.

In the fall, glorious colors abound while you enjoy a full country breakfast on the sunporch.

A roaring fire in the majestic Great Room, comfortable conversation while sipping your favorite "spirit," preparing for cross-country skiing or just taking in the breathtaking vista of a winter wonderland, make winter a pleasure at Glasbern.

The king and queen bedded guest rooms are appointed with classic, traditional furniture, highlighted with fine country accents. Each has the amenities of a fine hotel. A full country breakfast is included with your room.

The Farmhouse Suites are equipped with kitchenettes, and one has a wood burning stove. The Luxury Rooms and Suites in the Carriage House offer whirlpools and fireplaces in each unit.

OPEN:	Year round.
GUEST ROOMS:	19 guest rooms and suites, all with private baths, phone, TV, radio; some rooms with fireplaces and whirlpool.
RESTAURANT:	Breakfast only. No restaurant on premises. Restaurants nearby. Complimentary snacks upon arrival.
CREDIT CLUBS:	American Express, MasterCard, Visa
RECREATION:	Bicycling, boating, cross-country, skiing, fishing, jogging, walking paths, picnic area, ballooning, outdoor pool.
RESTRICTIONS:	No children, no pets
EXTRAS:	Meeting space
RATES:	$60-$125 per room, double occupancy. Includes breakfast. (Tax 6%)

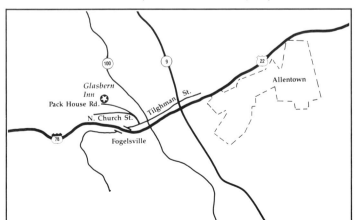

DIRECTIONS:
From the northeast extension of the Pennsylvania Turnpike, take Interstate 78/US 22 west to State Route 100 north. Turn left almost immediately onto Main (Tilghman) Street. Then turn right onto North Church Street, and take the right fork onto Pack House Road. The inn is three quarters of a mile after the fork.

**FOGELSVILLE
PENNSYLVANIA**

THE GUESTHOUSE AT DONECKERS

318-324 North State Street, Ephrata, Pennsylvania 17522

(717) 738-2421

Tucked into the hills of northern Lancaster County, this 19-room guesthouse is part of an unexpected country experience. The Doneckers Community includes a beautiful restaurant, offering classic and country French cuisine, and extensive fine fashion stores.

This turn-of-the-century home was charmingly restored to preserve much of its original architecture. Guest rooms are individually decorated with hand-stenciled walls, folk art, designer linens, and local antiques. Some rooms feature a fireplace and jacuzzi. Fresh flowers and fruit provide a warm greeting upon your arrival. The parlor beckons with cable TV, magazines and table games. At the day's end, you can retire to a cozy room.

Doneckers is near the largest antiques

market in the Northeast, historic Ephrata Cloister, Hershey, theaters, craft days, and the rolling farmlands of the Amish community.

Spring sets a beautiful stage for exploring, as the greening of "America's Garden Spot" begins. May blossoms announce the 4-month reign of the Renaissance Faire at Lancaster County's Mount Hope Winery.

Summer brings out the German heritage of the area as an authentic Bier Fest comes to life, June through September, 10 minutes north of the inn.

The clear, blue autumn sky is a lovely background for the turning of fall foliage. On a crisp October weekend, the sky will be dotted with dozens of colorful hot air balloons, racing for the title of the Lancaster County Hot Air Balloon Championships. September and October boast numerous county fairs in the surrounding farm communities. During the last week of September, Ephrata bustles with the activities of the largest street fair in Pennsylvania, complete with parade, amusement rides and exhibits of farm life. A true taste of rural America!

The first snowfall reminds us of the meaningful Holiday Season to come. The Guesthouse is decorated in holiday finery, adding a special warmth to our cozy accommodations. It's a perfect time to visit the Ephrata Cloister, a 16th century community that lives by strict religious principles, sheltered from the rest of the world. In December, the inn hosts several guided candlelight tours preceded by a delicious dinner in The Restaurant.

OPEN:	Year round
GUEST ROOMS:	19 guest rooms and suites, all with phones and work areas. 17 rooms with private baths. Some with fireplaces and jacuzzis.
RESTAURANT:	Buffet breakfast. Lunch and dinner served daily, closed Wednesdays. Extensive wine list.
CREDIT CARDS:	American Express, Carte Blanche, Diners Club, MasterCard, Visa
RECREATION:	Nearby: Crafts, antique shops, Amish Country, cross country skiing, lake, golf and historical sights.
RESTRICTIONS:	No pets
EXTRAS:	Meeting space, TV and games in parlor
RATES:	$69-$130 per room. Includes buffet breakfast. (Tax 6%)

DIRECTIONS:
Located between Lancaster and Reading off of Route 222 in the community of Doneckers on State Street

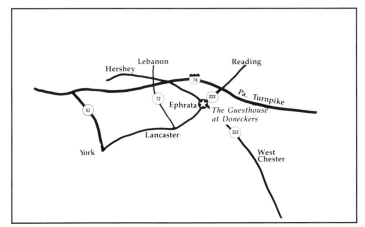

**EPHRATA
PENNSYLVANIA**

INN AT TURKEY HILL

991 Central Road, Bloomsburg, Pennsylvania 17815

(717) 387-1500

The award-winning Inn at Turkey Hill is nestled amidst the rolling hills and farmlands of central Pennsylvania where warm hospitality and exceptional cuisine prevail. The immaculate and beautifully designed complex is conveniently located near Bloomsburg, the only incorporated town in Pennsylvania.

Inn guests enjoy the famous flaming foliage during the fall and cross-country skiing and other sports during winter. During the spring, guests can tour dozens of covered bridges, and summer brings fishing in the many rivers and streams or touring state parks and gamelands. The nationally registered Bloomsburg Historic Architecture District, Bloomsburg University, and the professional Bloomsburg Theatre Ensemble delight visitors year round.

The main building of the Inn at Turkey Hill, built in 1839 as a private residence, has been in the Eyerly family since 1942. The family developed the white clapboard complex of guest rooms around the Main House in 1984, fulfilling the dream of the late Paul Eyerly, a prominent newspaper publisher and civic leader. Each modern, oversized Country Cottage is tastefully decorated with handmade furnishings from Georgia's

Habersham Plantations, european duvets, and fine toiletries. Suites also feature fireplaces and jacuzzis. Local and national newspapers accompany the complimentary continental breakfast in the glass-enclosed Greenhouse, or breakfast can be delivered to your room in a country basket.

The entire site is perfectly suited for relaxation. The guest rooms overlook a landscaped courtyard with a duckpond, seasonal flowers, gazebo, and walking paths.

Three superb dining rooms - the Mural Room, the Stencil Room, and the Green-house - feature the finest cuisine. Each combines exquisite dining with simple elegance and unreserved hospitality. Sunday brunch buffet features hand-carved roast beef and country ham and dozens of brunch entree favorites. Guests can relax in the Tavern, and during spring and summer the courtyard and patio provide a special setting for business or social occasions.

At this very affordable inn, the emphasis is on service. The personal touches and extra attention that typify the Inn at Turkey Hill are normally found only in expensive, world-class hotels. But here in rural Pennsylvania, both staff and setting extend warmth, comfort, charm, and hospitality.

OPEN:	Year round
GUEST ROOMS:	18 guest rooms and suites, all with private baths, phones, TVs. Some rooms with jacuzzi.
RESTAURANT:	Breakfast and dinner served daily. Small lounge.
RESTRICTIONS:	None
CREDIT CARDS:	American Express, MasterCard, Visa, Diners Club, Carte Blanche
EXTRAS:	Meeting space, children under 12 free, handicapped facilities, babysitting, no smoking rooms available.
RATES:	$50-$120 per room. Continental Breakfast included. (Tax 6%)

DIRECTIONS:
Located at Exit 35 off
Interstate 80.

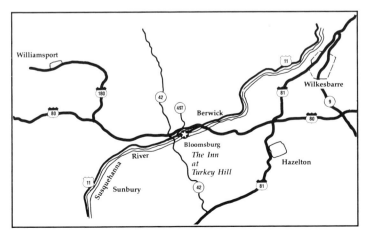

**BLOOMSBURG
PENNSYLVANIA**

MERCERSBURG INN

405 South Main Street, Mercersburg, Pennsylvania 17236

(717) 328-5231

Mercersburg's central location in the Cumberland Valley affords this rural community a surrounding countryside of rolling green fields and mountain views. Unhurried drives yield delightful destinations such as Harper's Ferry, the historical battlefields of Antietam and Gettysburg, and beautiful state parks with miles of hiking trails. Other recreational opportunities abound including hunting, fishing, golf, swimming, tennis and skiing.

The central portion of Mercersburg has been placed on the National Register of Historic Places and provides architectural delights from clapboard covered log homes of 1750 to the Georgian Revival grandeur of the Mercersburg Inn.

The Mercersburg Academy Chapel is the village's most distinctive landmark. Patterned after the great Gothic cathedrals of Europe, the chapel is part of the 300 acre Mercersburg Academy, a private, nonsectarian co-ed boarding school established in 1893 on the former site of Marshall College (now Franklin and Marshall College in Lancaster, PA). Designed by Ralph Adams Crain, at the time the most eminent church architect in America, the chapel features

49 intricate stained-glass windows commissioned from nine of the best stained-glass artists in America, England, and Ireland. It's 43 bell carillon creates a wonderfully rich musical accompaniment for strolls through the historical village and campus.

The chapel also becomes the center of attraction not only for the village and school but also for hundreds of people in the surrounding countryside when it becomes the host site of the community choral groups.

With the arrival of fall, the Cumberland Valley has the Tuscarora Mountains as a backdrop for the display of the fall foliage. Local craft and apple festivals create an abundance of country entertainment, dining, and shopping opportunities.

Located in the Southern portion of this village, perched upon Mercersburg's highest hill sits what was the private residence of Harry Byron. His home, built in 1910, is a 20,000 square foot Georgian Revival mansion surround by 5 ½ acres of grounds and was once known as "Prospect." Now the Mercersburg Inn, the mansion was the largest private home ever built in Southern Pennsylvania.

The inn's rooms are decorated with antiques and locally handmade king sized beds with four posters and canopies. Most rooms on the second floor feature porches or balconies, and some have working fireplaces.

With over 6,000 square feet of public rooms including a grand foyer with marble pillars and curving dual staircases,

the inn provides the unique setting for weddings, business retreats, or other special events.

A tradition of casual elegance in dining is continued today with the inn serving six course single entre meals that change each day. The cuisine is New American and features meats and vegetables produced locally for the inn at the chef's direction. Mornings at the inn bring aromas of Kona coffee and freshly baked breakfast breads. Dining is casual but features a two course breakfast.

OPEN:	Year round
GUEST ROOMS:	15 guest rooms, all with private bath and phones. A few with fireplaces and balconies.
RESTAURANT:	Full country breakfast, lunch and six course dinner served daily. Pub.
CREDIT CARDS:	MasterCard, Visa
RECREATION:	On premises: bicycles, checkers, pool table. Nearby: boating, cross-country and downhill skiing, fishing, jogging, lake and outdoor pool.
RESTRICTIONS:	No smoking in inn, no pets.
EXTRAS:	Meeting space, TV in lounge
RATES:	$65-$90 per person, double occupancy. Full Country Breakfast and six course dinner included. (Tax 6%)

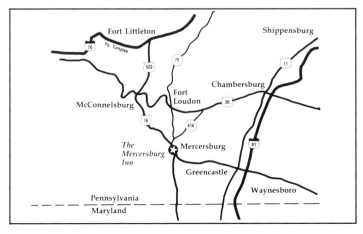

DIRECTIONS:
Route 70 to Route 16, inn is on Main Street.

MERCERSBURG
PENNSYLVANIA

1740 HOUSE

River Road, Lumberville, Pennsylvania 18933
(215) 297-5661

An 18th century farm on the banks of the Delaware River in historic Bucks County is the site of the 1740 House, built by Janet and Harry Nessler to embody their idea of the perfect country inn. In a quiet setting among the trees, each of the inn's guest rooms has a balcony or terrace overlooking the river and the canal. The rooms are appointed with carefully selected Early American furnishings, with interesting blends of old and new.

The dining room provides splendid views of the river, along with fine and abundant food. The innkeepers offer privacy and seclusion to their guests, as well as suggestions for side trips and excursions. Bucks County has a wealth of historic and natural treasures, one of which is the well-known town of New Hope, seven miles away.

Convenient to New York, Washington, DC and Philadelphia, Bucks County is well known for its covered bridges, fine restaurants, charming villages with antique stores and artisan boutiques.

This rustic inn is a perfect location for quiet moments of contemplation or to serve as a home base for avid antiquers and outdoor sports enthusiasts. With ice-skating, sledding and skiing close at hand, winter is active in Bucks County. During warmer months there is fishing, canoeing, boating and a swimming pool on the premises. And in the autumn, the vivid fall foliage is a favorite for weekenders.

You find that well in advance reservations are required at the 1740 House during peak times.

The invitation from the 1740 House is "If you can't be a house guest in Bucks County, be ours."

OPEN:	Year round
GUEST ROOMS:	24 guest rooms, all with private baths.
RESTAURANT:	Breakfast and dinner served. No dinner on Sunday or Monday.
CREDIT CARDS:	NONE
RECREATION:	On premises: outdoor pool. Nearby: golf, fishing, antiquing and historical sites.
RESTRICTIONS:	No handicapped facilities, no children, no pets. Minimum stay on some holidays and weekends.
EXTRAS:	Meeting space
RATES:	$65-$78 per room, double occupancy. Buffet breakfast included. (Tax 6%)

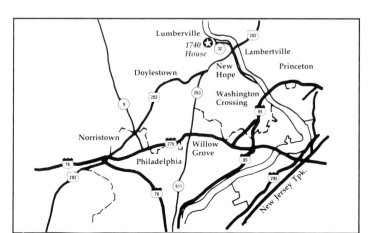

DIRECTIONS:
From I-95, take the New Hope-Yardley Exit and follow State Route 32, north. The 1740 House is six and a half miles north of the New Hope traffic light.

**LUMBERVILLE
PENNSYLVANIA**

MILL STREET INN

75 Mill Street, Newport, Rhode Island 02840

(401) 849-9500

If you're considering a trip to New England don't miss visiting Newport, Rhode Island. The Atlantic Ocean and its rocky coast provide the backdrop for this historic port city of restored homes, unique shops, galleries, excellent restaurants and, of course, lobster. A moderate climate allows visitors to pursue outdoor and indoor activities year round.

Come to Newport in the spring and enjoy the fresh greens of a new beginning. You can visit the mansions open for touring in April, or rent a bicycle for a spectacular ride on Ocean Drive. Sailing regattas start in May and continue through October. You can follow the races from the rocks near Brenton Reef.

Summertime offers beachcombing, fishing, sailing, clambakes, and a variety of festivals. The Volvo and Virginia Slims Tennis Championships are in July as well as the annual kite and folk festivals. August brings the famed Jazz Festival to Ft. Adams where greats and near-greats perform every year. Special outdoor concerts and the mansion recital series are also available for music lovers.

After Labor Day the days are less hectic, the weather still gorgeous and the boat shows are in full swing. Choose the yacht of your dreams at the sail, power or wooden boat extravaganzas. Leisurely wander through the many antique stores on Franklin and Spring Streets.

The winter season is a peaceful time with warm shops, the smell of spice in the air and daily activities of the month-long Christmas in Newport celebration.

To capture the flavor and fun of Newport, you'll want to stay in the harbor area. Mill Street Inn, a 19th century sawmill renovated in 1984, is ideally located for browsing or strolling the harbor area. The original brick structure is well known to local Aquidneck Islanders who needed sawdust for their pets. Listed on the National Register of Historic Places, the inn opened in 1985 and is an innovative blend of old and new. Dramatic contemporary interiors set off old brick and beams. The striking nautical white pipe railing of the lobby stairs is the perfect building accent in a city with such a rich relationship to ships and the sea.

Each suite features a bedroom with queen bed, living room with sofa sleeper, easy chairs, color TV, radio, ceiling

fans, individual heat control, and full tiled bath. Exposed brick walls are in sharp contrast to modern overstuffed furnishings of soft greys, reds and whites. Townhouse suites offer a wet bar and/or private deck with a terrific view of Narragansett Bay. For an especially romantic atmosphere, stay in townhouse –210 with its stunning red spiral staircase.

OPEN:	Year round
GUEST ROOMS:	23 suites, all with private baths, phones and TVs, some with private decks and wet bars. Some townhouse style.
RESTAURANT:	Continental breakfast and afternoon tea. Restaurants nearby.
CREDIT CARDS:	American Express, Carte Blanche, Diners Club, MasterCard, Visa
RECREATION:	Nearby: bicycles, boating, fishing, golf, jogging, walking paths, picnic area, ocean, sailing, tennis, racquetball, antiquing and art museums.
RESTRICTIONS:	No pets
EXTRAS:	Handicapped facilities
RATES:	$75-$165 per room. Includes continental breakfast. (Tax 10%)

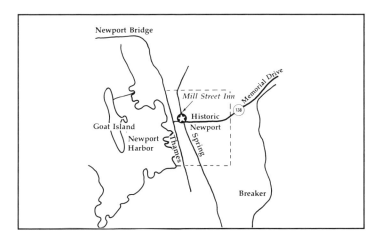

DIRECTIONS:
From North: Route 93S to Route 24, then onto Route 114 or Route 138. Follow directly into Newport. Then left onto Thames Street. As far as you can go, left onto Mill Street, one block (stop), 3rd building on right. From South: Route 195 to Route 24 and then to Route 114.

NEWPORT
RHODE ISLAND

MAISON DUPRE

317 East Bay Street, Charleston, South Carolina 29401

(803) 723-8691

Maison DuPre, "The Inn of Historic Elegance," circa 1804, is in the downtown Ansonborough Historic District of charming Charleston, South Carolina. The owners and innkeepers, Lucille and Bob Mulholland, restored three 1800's Charleston "Single Houses" and two Carriage Houses to create their inn.

"Every room has an Oriental carpet. They're the palettes from which I obtain my colors and inspiration when I'm decorating the rooms." Lucille's own evocative pastels, watercolors, and oil paintings of landscapes and still-lifes are hung throughout the inn in all of the guest rooms, along with prints of the French artists of the impressionist era. Their warm blues, roses, apricots, golds, beiges, and creams are repeated in draperies and linens, creating the feeling that you are walking into a French Impressionist painting. Hardly surprising when you discover that Mrs. Mulholland's favorite artists include Monet and Renoir. Throughout the inn are artistic contributions by the Mulholland family.

The inn's gracefully weathered frame and brick buidings and sun-washed, flower-scented courtyards with three flowing fountains, all surrounded by tall garden walls and wrought-iron gates, welcome their guests to step back into early Colonial times and relax.

All rooms have marble and tile baths with brass fittings, antique armoirs, oriental carpets and antiques. An executive suite, "Honeymoon Suites", Carriage House kitchen suite, and twelve other guest rooms with queen-size "Charleston Rice Beds", and pencil post twin peds, some with canopys, all create a feeling that at any moment Rhett Butler and Scarlett O'Hara may come into view!

Guests enjoy a Continental breakfast, "Low-Country Tea" each afternoon, turndown service and chocolate, a paper delivered to their door, and a carriage

ride of the historic district!

Maison DuPre, is the perfect place to stay when visiting Charleston, "the most European city in the United States". The city abounds in historic sites and fine restaurants and has an excellent downtown shopping area with many fine antique shops. From its beautiful harbour the first shot of the Civil War was fired at Fort Sumter. The beautiful homes of the historic district survived the Revolutionary War, the Civil War, earthquakes, and hurricanes.

Maison DuPre is also an excellent location for small meetings, parties, receptions, and weddings. Meetings accommodations include a lavishly appointed dining/meeting room and a drawingroom with a baby grand piano.

Maison DuPre received a Carolopolis Award denoting houses of historic importance, from the Preservation Society of Charleston.

OPEN:	Year round
GUEST ROOMS:	16 guest rooms and suites, all with private baths, phones, TVs and nightly turn-down service.
RESTAURANT:	Continental breakfast served and "Low Country Tea party" in the afternoon. Horse and buggy available to nearby restaurants. Beer and wine available.
CREDIT CARDS:	American Express, Visa, MasterCard
RECREATION:	Nearby: sailing, boating, crafts, antiques and historic sights.
RESTRICTIONS:	No pets
EXTRAS:	Meeting space
RATES:	$82.50-$200 per room. Continental breakfast included. (Tax 7%)

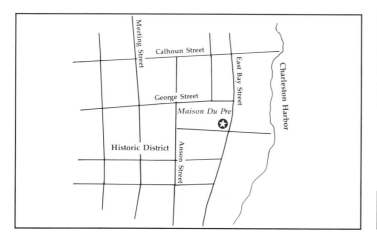

DIRECTIONS:
From North and West, I-26 to East Bay Street, downtown to George Street. From South and East, Route 17 across Ashley River to Calhoun Street to East Bay to George Street.

CHARLESTON
SOUTH CAROLINA

WASHINGTON SCHOOL INN

P.O. Box 536, Park City, Utah 84060

(800) 824-1672 (801) 649-3800

Sitting high in the Wasatch Mountains, Park City was founded as a mining camp and blossomed into a boom town in the western tradition. In 1889, the Washington School opened to serve the growing needs of school-aged children in Park City. From then until 1931, the school was home to thousands

features as the bell tower topped by a flag pole, the dormer windows of pediment shape and the three-by-nine-foot school house windows.

The inn is a true artisan's delight with rich hardwoods throughout, hand etched glass, and myriad fabrics. Each of the suites is individually appointed to create a luxurious but comfortable ambience. Every detail has a been considered to ensure relaxation in a beautiful setting. Here, service may be grace and good manners to leave you peacefully to yourself, or cater to whatever whim suits your fancy.

Today, Park City has become a world class ski and summer resort. After a long day on the slopes come back to the inn to relax and unwind in the jacuzzi or sauna. Then, dinner and all the entertainment Park City has to offer are yours. Before retiring, enjoy a late-night mint left on your pillow.

of students. It changed hands in the mid-1930's and eventually fell into a state of disrepair.

In June 1985, the fully refurbished Washington School Inn was dedicated as Park City's premier country inn. Now on the Utah Register and the National Register of Historic Places, the exterior has been restored with such distinctive

OPEN:	Closed May
GUEST ROOMS:	15 guest rooms and suites, all with private baths and phones. Some rooms with TVs, radios, and fireplaces.
RESTAURANT:	Breakfast lunch and dinner served daily. High tea with wine and cheese in the afternoon.
CREDIT CARDS:	American Express, MasterCard, Visa
RECREATION:	On premises: jacuzzi, sauna. Nearby: bicycles, cross-country and downhill skiing, tennis, racquetball, golf, jogging, fishing, indoor and outdoor pool, horseback riding.
RESTRICTIONS:	No children under 12, no pets.
EXTRAS:	Meeting space

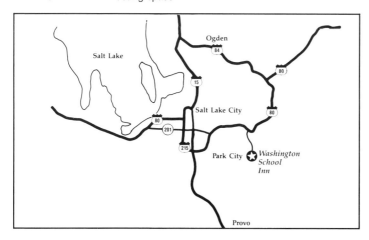

RATES: $75-$225 per room. Complimentary full breakfast. (Tax 9.5%)

DIRECTIONS: From I-80, take Park City exit onto Route 248. Go seven miles to the inn at 544 Park Avenue.

PARK CITY UTAH

THE BLACK BEAR INN

Mountain Road, Bolton Valley, Vermont 05477

(802) 434-2126

The Black Bear Inn, the only country inn located at the Bolton Valley Ski and Summer Resort in northern Vermont, is a lovely complement to the resort's hotel and condominiums and is a fine example of a traditional New England inn.

In the heart of the beautiful Green Mountains, midway between Burlington and Montpelier, the Black Bear Inn is close to Vermont's most popular attractions. Spring through fall, enjoy tennis, cycling, horseback riding, antiquing, golf, trout fising, theatre, canoeing, and country auctions nearby. Visit the Shelburne Museum with its world-renowned collection of Americana. Then take a sightseeing cruise on the blue waters of Lake Champlain. While at the inn, swim in the heated outdoor pool or hike along miles of enchanting woodland trails. Ex-

perience Vermont's fall foliage as autumn sets the mountains ablaze with brilliant colors. Winter brings its own special kind of exicitement to the Valley. The Black Bear Inn is now New England's only slopeside country inn, with both cross-country and downhill skiing right from its door. The resort's two mountains, designed for all levels of ability, boast 39 alpine runs, five lifts, and extensive snowmaking, as well as 100 kilometers of breathtaking cross-country ski trails. Just steps away from the inn is a full facility sports complex with an indoor pool and tennis courts, sauna, jacuzzi, exercise room and tanning beds.

Favored by many for its European charm, the homelike ambience of the inn is an expression of the personal tastes of its owners and innkeepers, Sue and Phil McKinnis. Sue, an avid antique hunter,

has given each of the inn's 24 rooms its own unique character. Patterned wallpaper, wing back chairs, antique bureaus and nightstands, and puffy handmade quilts all combine to make the inn a quaint and cozy home-away-from-home. All rooms have a private bath and color television and many have balconies offering panoramic mountain views. In cooler months, guests are greeted by the glow and warmth of a large woodburning stove and the scent of hot spiced cider in the inn's great room. The Black Bear Inn's plant-filled sunroom, overlooking the terraced garden, is the perfect place to relax with a book or chat with friends over breakfast.

The dining area is intimate, and guests have the opportunity to get acquainted and share stories while enjoying one of a variety of different nightly entrees, all strictly fresh and homemade. A sample of these include Veal du Maison, Baked Stuffed Shrimp, Breast of Chicken Suzanne, Steak au Poivre and Rack of Lamb Dijonaise. Fresh herbs from the inn's own garden are used extensively. Hearty Vermont country breakfasts are highlighted by homemade muffins and pastries, baked fresh every day. And always, there is the sweet aroma of baking breads wafting from the kitchen. Breakfast and dinner are served daily. During the summer a Sunday brunch is offered poolside and lunch is available in the winter on weekends and holidays.

OPEN:	May - October and Mid-December - March
GUEST ROOMS:	24 guest rooms and suites, all with private baths and TV's.
RESTAURANT:	Continental country breakfast served daily. Candlelight dinner served at 7:00 pm, dress is casual. Lunch-winter season, during holiday weeks and on weekends.
CREDIT CARDS:	Visa, MasterCard
RECREATION:	Boating, canoeing, downhill and cross country skiing, fishing, golf, sailing and tennis
RESTRICTIONS:	No pets, no handicapped facilities, no phones in guest rooms
EXTRAS:	Outdoor pool, babysitter, meeting room, 24 hour emergency phone contact available

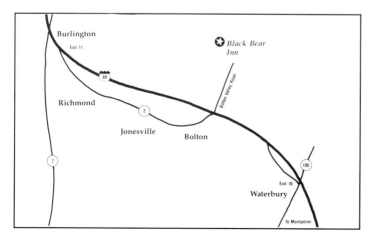

RATES:
$59-$99 per night room only. Add $25 per person per day for full breakfast and dinner. (Tax 6%)

DIRECTIONS:
Just an easy five-minute drive from I-89 and less than half an hour from Burlington's International Airport or 15 minutes from the Amtrak depot.

BOLTON VALLEY VERMONT

INN AT WEATHERSFIELD

Route 106, P.O. Box 165, Weathersfield, Vermont 05151
(802) 263-9217

eleven scenic acres. An English garden with trellis highlights the west end lawn, and a traditional kitchen garden with herbs and vegetables is on the northwest side. An amphitheatre with stage and carpeted log seats for nearly 100 persons is tucked away in the woods and is used for weddings, band concerts, and small theatre groups.

The guest rooms and suites each have their own style and mood ranging from Colonial to Empire and Victorian. One room, for example, has a big brass bed with canopy, an Empire love seat from President Grant's home, and an oak wash stand from Sears and Roebuck's late 1800's catalog. All rooms have special features like colonial rockers, hand stitched quilts, and four poster, canopy or brass beds. Seven of the guest rooms have working fireplaces, and some have private balconies with a view of Hawks Mountain. All baths have perfumed soaps, dried flowers, and soft bath towels.

An afternoon "high English" tea is served in the parlor by overflowing bookshelves and a stone fireplace. Mary Louise's imaginative meals draw devotees from around the world. Ron plays the piano, inviting guests to make requests from Broadway shows, standards and 'golden oldies'.

A friendly horse named Richard has been in residence at the inn for the past five years, and with a little help from Honey, a 300 pound Shetland pony, sufficient "horsepower" is available for sleigh and carriage rides. A recreational field has been set up on the inn's old ten-

At the end of a maple tree-lined drive, off a hilly country road, you will discover the Inn at Weathersfield, an eighteenth century mansion surrounded by tall pines and cared for by Mary Louise and Ron Thorburn. The inn features rooms furnished with exquisite antiques, well-kept grounds, excellent individually prepared meals, and a friendly atmosphere.

The inn is situated in the center of

mels and peels. At Thanksgiving and on other special occasions, Mary Louise masterminds a complete dinner using these early cooking facilities, all with the innkeepers and staff in period attire.

Recreational activities abound in this area, with some to the best hiking trails on nearby Ascutney Mountain, the tallest free standing mountain east of the Mississippi River. Six major areas for downhill skiing can be reached within 30 minutes driving time. Groomed cross-country trails, are also easily accessible. Augustus St. Gauden's home and studio (America's most famous sculptor), Robert Todd Lincoln's home, the Billings Farm and Museum (A working dairy farm and museum depicting life in Vermont 100 years ago), President Calvin Coolidge's birthplace and summer White House, and the Weston Priory, where 'the singing monks' hold inspirational services on a daily basis, are all nearby.

nis court. Here guests may play volleyball, badminton, croquet, or horseshoes.

The inn has original 18th Century cooking hearths, beehive bake oven, reflector ovens, spider pots, trivets, tram-

---

OPEN:	Year round
GUEST ROOMS:	12 guest rooms, all with private baths. 24 hour phone service available. Some rooms have fireplaces.
RESTAURANT:	Breakfast and dinner served. Late afternoon high tea including wine, sherry and special foods.
CREDIT CARDS:	American Express, MasterCard, Visa
RECREATION:	On premises: library, indoor games, sauna, walking and jogging paths. Nearby: hot tubs, skiing, picnic areas, racquetball, lake, crafts, antiquing and tours of local attractions.
RESTRICTIONS:	No pets, no children under 8 years old.
EXTRAS:	Meeting space, babysitter

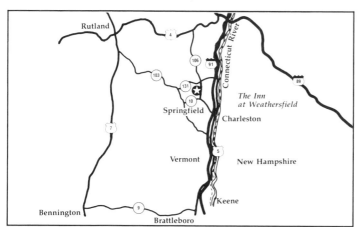

The Inn at Weathersfield

RATES: $140-$150 per room, double occupancy. Breakfast, high tea, and dinner included. (Tax 6%)

DIRECTIONS: From North, I-91 to Exit 8, turn onto Route 131 West to Route 106S, 4.5 miles to inn. From South, I-91 North to Exit 7, turn onto Route 106NW to inn (9.5 miles).

WEATHERSFIELD VERMONT

MOUNTAIN TOP INN

Mountain Top Road, Chittenden, Vermont 05737
(802) 483-2311

Nestled in the picturesque Green Mountains of central Vermont and secluded on a 1000 acre estate, Mountain Top Inn commands a spectacular view of the lake and surrounding mountains. This warm New England country inn, steeped in the area's finest tradition, has been referred to as "Vermont's best kept secret."

Entering the inn, guests are welcomed by a spacious lobby of post and beam construction, an old stone fireplace, many antiques and a panoramic vista that will never be forgotten. Down the glass enclosed semicircular stairs, one encounters a charming candlelight dining room where excellence of cuisine and service are renowned.

The guest rooms are well appointed in the fine New England tradition. Most of these rooms have breathtaking views of the lake and mountains. Also available are cottage and chalet units within a short distance of the inn, many with a fireplace or woodstove and lovely views.

Nearby, one may relax in the private

sauna and whirlpool room. The recreation room with billiards, table tennis, foosball and speed hockey table is for all to enjoy. Upstairs, the library and reading lobby offer restful solitude and the Breezeway Gift Shop provides a delightful diversion.

While maintaining the charming qualities of a quaint country inn, Mountain Top Inn offers all of the activities of the finest resorts. Sail, canoe, windsurf and fish on the crystal clear 650 acre lake surrounded by mountains which provide the perfect tranquil setting for these water sports. Take the 12 person pontoon boat for guided lake excursions and trips to lakeside breakfasts. Swim in and sun by the mountain lake or enjoy the heated outdoor pool and sun terrace.

Horseback ride on miles of scenic trails. For the less adventuresome, try the horsedrawn wagon rides. Play tennis in a most scenic setting overlooking lake and mountains on an all-weather court.

Walk up the road to the Farm and visit the Sugar House where, in the spring, the maple syrup is made for the inn, or hike on Mountain Top's 1000 acres and adjacent National Forest land. Follow the trail from the front door of the inn to the Long Trail and Appalachian Trail or hike to Mount Carmel. If you are a cross-country skier, you will revel at the Mountain Top Inn, an official training center for the U.S. Nordic Ski Team.

The inn's central location provides easy access to Vermont's winter activities. Killington and Pico Alpine Ski Areas are just minutes away. Nearby, one can find winter carnivals, indoor ice skating, tennis, racquetball, swimming and health spas. Guests of the inn have complimentary membership at Centre Sport, the area's finest indoor pool and fitness facility.

OPEN:	Year round
GUEST ROOMS:	33 rooms, including 15 cottages and chalets, all with private baths and phones.
RESTAURANT:	Full breakfast, lunch and dinner are available. Lounge.
CREDIT CARDS:	American Express, Visa
RECREATION:	On premises: boating, cross country skiing, fishing, golf, hot tubs, jacuzzi, running and walking paths, picnic areas, sailing, sauna and lake.
RESTRICTIONS:	No pets
EXTRAS:	Babysitting, meeting space, handicap facilities
RATES:	$65-$142 rooms, $72-$157 cottages, per person based on double occupancy. Rates are seasonal and include breakfast and dinner. Other package plans also available. (Tax 6%)

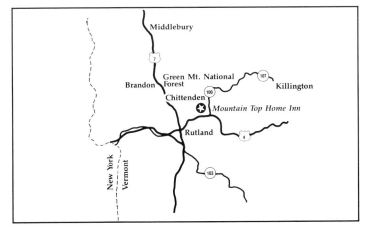

DIRECTIONS
Near Rutland, accessible from U.S. Route 4 and 7. Call for detailed directions.

CHITTENDEN VERMONT

RABBIT HILL INN

Pucker Street, Lower Waterford, Vermont 05848

(802) 748-5168

In the uppermost portion of Vermont are 2,000 square miles known as the Northeast Kingdom, which, simply put, is an American treasure. This is a place where the seasons of the year are as distinct as the primary colors. Life is rugged and, in a sense, mirrors the land: resistant to time, and magnificent in its beauty. Just above the Connecticut River is a tiny hamlet virtually untouched for more than 150 years. It is named the White Village (every building painted white with green shutters,) and is reputed to be Vermont's most photographed village. Here sits the classic country inn known as Rabbit Hill. This inn has been part of the commerce and hospitality of Vermont since 1795.

Today it boasts two magnificently restored buildings (the second dating 1825). Of note are the five porches, two of which are supported by solid pine Doric pillars. There are wide pine floor boards, and eight fireplaces. Antiques and quality reproduction furnishings from New England abound.

Guests are welcomed into the Federal Period parlor for afternoon tea and freshly baked treats. There is a pub called the Snooty Fox, which has a full service bar, and a candlelit dining room with beautifully crafted pine tables. In winter, a woodstove warms the Gift Shop and After-Sports-Lounge. You are likely to find chili, popcorn or cocoa for your enjoyment and warmth. Fresh lemonade and penny candy are the fare in warmer months. Individually decorated guest chambers have motifs such as antique letters, hat boxes and bonnets, or reproduction wooden toys. One room is based on the life of a 1900's woman named Clara, and another, the Music Chamber, boasts a working pump organ.

Dining, food presentation, and music are given tremendous consideration at the inn. The menu changes daily and the evening meal is prepared only after your order is placed. It is seasoned with herbs and garnished with flowers grown in the inn's gardens. The cream used is fresh from the local farm collective. The maple syrup, an ingredient in the inn's coveted salad dressing, is from a neighbor's sugaring operation.

Located within twelve minutes of the inn in opposite directions are the towns of St. Johnsbury, Vermont and Littleton, New Hampshire. These towns offer art galleries and specialty shops. Antiquing and driving tours are laid out for you by the innkeepers so that you may explore rural Vermont at its best. Two downhill ski areas are within easy reach: Cannon

Mountain, 20 minutes away in New Hampshire, and Burke Mountain, 35 minutes away in Vermont.

Rabbit Hill is a quiet and gentle place with a personal and caring touch. The superb attention to detail has resulted in an elegant country home that is crisp and fresh. This is a romantic inn where you are likely to mark time by the movement of the sun. Its setting has a Brigadoon-like quality. Here the rural life persists, survival is not taken for granted, and people cultivate their individuality as well as their crops.

OPEN:	Year round except closed April and first 3 weeks of November.
GUEST ROOMS:	18 guest rooms and suites, all with private baths and radios. Some with fireplaces and TVs.
RESTAURANT:	Breakfast and dinner served daily. After-Sports-Lounge and Pub. Operating schedule same as inn.
CREDIT CARDS:	MasterCard, Visa
RECREATION:	Nearby: bicycling, picnic areas, cross country skiing, fishing, swimming, canoeing, jogging, hiking, crafts, antiquing and historical sights.
RESTRICTIONS:	No pets, no smoking. No children under the age of 10.
EXTRAS:	Babysitting, meeting space.
RATES:	$55-$90 per person, double occupancy, plus 15% gratuity. Breakfast, tea time and dinner included. (Tax 6%)

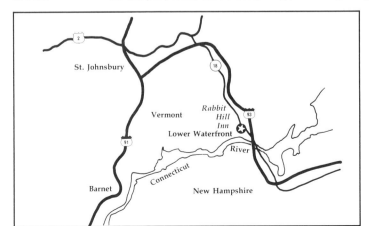

DIRECTIONS:
The inn is on Route 18, almost midway between St. Johnsbury, VT and Littleton, NH. From Route I-91 onto I-93. Take Exit 1 and follow Route 18 seven miles south.

WAITSFIELD INN

Box 969, Waitsfield, Vermont 05673

(802) 496-3979

The Waitsfield Inn offers gracious lodging and dining in an elegant 1825 parsonage located in central Vermont. In the heart of the Mad River Valley, surrounded by the Green Mountains, the inn is only 15 minutes from the Sugarbush and Mad River Glen ski areas. Together these premier ski centers offer a hundred runs of all degrees of challenge. For cross-country skiers, there are numerous trails and centers nearby. And who could resist a ride in a horse drawn sleigh?

In warmer weather, nearby activities are endless. Hiking the Long Trail or the beautiful hills nearby, cycling, fishing, swimming, golf, tennis, horseback rid-

ing, soaring or antiquing are all popular. Located in the village, the inn is within walking distance of interesting shops, boutiques, craft centers and country stores.

The inn was originally built as a family home in 1825 and later it became a church parsonage. Through the years it has been a tavern and a ski dormitory. All of the guest rooms are individually furnished with antiques, hand-made comforters, and are traditionally warm and gracious.

The common room is in the old barn, added to the house in 1835. Its original wood planked flooring, walls and ceiling provide a most welcome spot to

snooze before the fire, to gather with other guests for conversation, to curl up with a book, or to enjoy a cocktail or a glass of wine from the full-service bar. A more intimate sitting room, also with a fireplace, is the converted wood shed. Tastefully furnished and delightfully cozy, it is a perfect location for that second cup of coffee, an evening nightcap, or a cup of mulled cider.

At the Waitsfield Inn, eating well is an important part of your visit. The dining room is located on the ground floor of the original house, retaining the original floor plan. The resulting smaller dining rooms are intimate and romantic, every table graced by the soft glow of an oil lamp.

The fare is continental with traditional favorites and a selection of imaginative and delicious entrees changing nightly. Guests rave about the roast duckling, fabulous fresh seafood dishes,

and the irrestible desserts.

Service is attentive, friendly, and personal. The inn is family owned and managed, providing the attention to detail and personal service which makes a real country inn so special. Every guest is provided a full breakfast and a choice of entree at dinner as part of their stay.

OPEN:	Year round
GUEST ROOMS:	16 guest rooms, all with private baths. Some with fireplaces. Phone service available.
RESTAURANT:	Full breakfast and dinner served daily and brunch on Sunday. Lunch served on special occasions only. Full bar service available.
CREDIT CARDS:	MasterCard, Visa
RECREATION:	Nearby: antiquing, boutiques and specialty shops, skiing, tennis, hiking, swimming, and golf.
RESTRICTIONS:	No pets, no children under 10 years old.
EXTRAS:	Meeting space

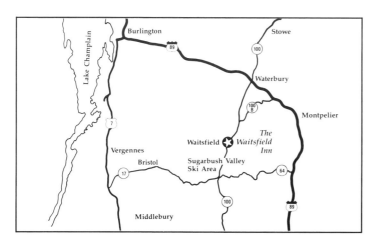

RATES: $50-$75 per person, double occupancy. Breakfast and dinner included. Gratuity of 15%. (Tax 6%)

DIRECTIONS: Leave I87, the New York State Thruway, at Exit 23. Follow US4 east to State Route 100, then go north to Waitsfield. The inn is on 100, just past the intersection with State Route 17.

WAITSFIELD VERMONT

WHITE HOUSE OF WILMINGTON

Route 9, Wilmington, Vermont 05363

(802) 464-2135

Set on the crest of a high, rolling hill, and surrounded by towering hardwoods and formal flower gardens, the White House of Wilmington stands, readily revealing why it has been said to be one of the most romantic places in the world. Built as a summer home in 1915 for the wealthy lumber baron, Martin Brown, the magnificent structure -- with its crafted French doors, two-storied terraces supported by soaring pillars, and ten fireplaces -- is as timeless and lovely as the Green Mountains which surround it.

From the large, open hearth in the entrance hall to the Victorian brass and crystal light fixtures that abound at the inn, the feeling of turn-of-the-century grandeur is ever-present. The original hardwood floors cover both the first and second stories of the inn. They are offset by beautiful woodwork, period antiques and even some of the home's original wallpaper that was printed in France in 1912.

The living room runs the entire width of the building and has as its centerpiece a massive and inviting fireplace. Here you can gather for relaxed activities such as friendly conversation, reading or playing some of the various games that are on hand. At one end of the room, French doors open onto one of the lower, front balconies where you can sit at wrought iron tables, sip a cocktail and take in the secluded mountain environment.

The three intimate dining rooms serve a collage of classic Continental dishes. The extensive menu is meticulously prepared, fresh, to please the most demanding gourmet.

The inn's guest rooms are beautifully furnished with antique dressers, period print wallpaper and country furnishings. Of the twelve guest rooms, five have working fireplaces (including one suite).

The large, lower level transformed into a refreshing and invigorating health spa includes whirlpool and sauna baths, sun tan room, and an indoor, heated swimming pool.

In addition to outstanding downhill skiing at nearby Mount Snow, a highly rated cross-country touring center, with 22 kilometers of groomed trails over high meadows and forested valleys is nearby. The trails range from novice to advanced and certified instructors are on hand to provide you with any necessary aid and advice. Facilities include a full service rental shop.

The White House's southern Vermont location is ideal for enjoying the numerous four-season activities in the area. Canoeing, fishing, power boating, and

waterskiing are available at Lake Whiteingham just 5 minutes away, as is horseback riding, antiquing and Vermont crafts. Historic sites such as the Bennington Battlefield and the internationally famous Marlboro Music Festival are within ½ hour drive. Of course, fall foliage is always a highlight.

OPEN:	Year round
GUEST ROOMS:	12 guest rooms, all private baths. 4 rooms with fireplaces. 1 suite with fireplace. 2 rooms with balconies and mountain views.
RESTAURANT:	3 dining rooms serving breakfast and dinner. Skiers' lunch in winter. Sunday brunch. Lounge.
CREDIT CARDS:	None accepted.
RECREATION:	On premises: cross country skiing, hot tubs, jogging, sauna, picnic area. Nearby: bicycles, boating, fishing, golf, lake, antiquing.
RESTRICTIONS:	No handicap facilities, no children under 10 years, no pets
EXTRAS:	Meeting space
RATES:	$160-$200 per room. Breakfast and dinner included for two people. (Tax 6%)

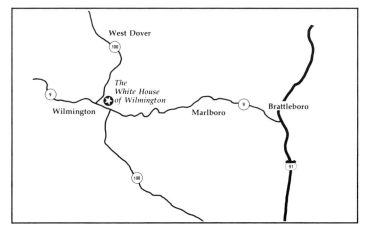

DIRECTIONS:
In southern Vermont on Route 9, 20 minutes west of Brattleboro. The Inn is on the right, just before entering town.

WILMINGTON VERMONT

BELLE GRAE INN

515 West Frederick Street, Staunton, Virginia 24401

(703) 886-5151

In the foothills of the Blue Ridge Mountains, the Belle Grae Inn sits in a quiet downtown neighborhood of Staunton. A restored historic Victorian mansion, the inn offers its guests an adventure into the past while enjoying all the amenities of today.

For relaxing after a day of antiquing, or enjoying the lovely Virginia countryside, the inn offers a veranda and courtyard with plenty of wicker rockers. During the winter months, guests enjoy

the parlour, sitting, and music rooms with their seven fireplaces. Tea and sherry are served each afternoon.

The Belle Grae Inn offers diners a choice of formal or informal settings. In the restored Victorian dining room, meals are elegantly served from a continental menu. A fine wine list is available to complement your meal. For a lighter meal, The Bistro is open to both guests of the inn and local residents. Here you will find fresh seafood, salads, pastas and a variety of local favorites. The Bistro is also a great place to gather with old friends or make new friends and enjoy your favorite beverage.

In Staunton you can visit Woodrow Wilson's Birthplace, the campus of Mary Baldwin College, the Statler Brothers Museum, or the 1901 Augusta County Courthouse. If antiquing is your interest, there are over 100 dealers in the Staunton area. For sports enthusiasts, there are three 18-hole PGA golf courses, tennis courts, swimming and nearby skiing. You won't want to miss listening to the Stonewall Brigade Band, America's oldest continously performing band, every Monday evening during the summer.

OPEN:	Year round
GUEST ROOMS:	12 rooms and suites, all private baths. Some with telephones, TVs, canopy beds and fireplaces.
RESTAURANT:	Formal Dining Room open for dinner on weekends. Bistro open breakfast, lunch and dinner. Lounge. Dining in the garden available weather permitting.
RECREATION:	Nearby: golf, swimming, tennis, skiing.
RESTRICTIONS:	No pets, no children younger than nine.
EXTRAS:	Inn dog - Belleboy.
RATES:	$55-$140 per room, double occupancy. Includes breakfast and afternoon tea. (Tax 7.5%)

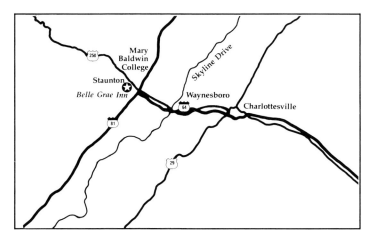

DIRECTIONS:
From North or South, I-81 to Exit 57. West to 250W to Route 254 West to 515 West, Frederick. From East or West, I-64 to I-81 North to Exit 57 to Route 250 West to 254 W to 515W. Frederick.

STAUNTON
VIRGINIA

JORDAN HOLLOW FARM

Route 2, Box 375, Stanley, Virginia 22851

(703) 778-2285

Marley Beers, a planning consultant, traveled the world and, while in Africa, she met her Dutch husband, Jetze. They now own and operate the historic Jordan Hollow Farm Inn in the Shenandoah Valley. The 45 acre site has a cluster of farm buildings on a 200-year-old Colonial horse farm. Many guests come here to ride horseback on trails crossing the farm into the foothills of the Shenandoah National Park.

The "Farmhouse Restaurant" has four dining rooms, two of which have hand-adzed log walls dating to 1790. Over the years the restaurant has had several additions, having been originally two houses which were joined by the construction of a second story with veranda and small pillars. The food is a blend of country and continental. Entrees such as Rainbow Trout, Roasted Quail, Rib

Eye Steak, and Pasta dishes are always available. Fresh fruits, vegetables, home baked bread and desserts are plentiful. The present pub/lounge, named "The Watering Trough," is a converted barn, with sidewalk cafe umbrellas, tables and chairs inviting guests to enjoy the sweeping view of the Blue Ridge Mountains. Inside the pub at night, twinkling candles light many small tables where guests enjoy refreshments from a full-service bar. A talented musician plays the piano for weekend entertainment which includes sing-a-longs led by the host, spontaneous dancing or animated conversations of the guests. At this inn everybody talks to everybody!

Built in 1983 to blend quietly into the scene, "Rowe's Lodge" has 16 bedrooms, all with private baths, central heating and air conditioning. A sun deck sur-

rounds the building offering serious porch sitters a lovely view of mountains, trees and horses grazing on rolling pastures.

Rowe's Lodge also has a conference room which can seat 40 people or may be divided into two breakout rooms. These training facilities are professionally designed and equipped to serve a variety of needs. Participants have said, "It's almost like having a conference at home...it's not like a hotel. During breaks we can sit on the porch, take a walk in the meadow, ride a horse or en-joy a picnic graciously organized by your staff on a moment's notice. What a wonderful combination of hard work and recreation."

The "Livery Ltd." is located in the 150-year-old bank barn where a variety of horses are available for beginner and advanced trail rides, Western or English saddles, in the meadows and mountains surrounding the farm. Several driving horses and ponies are often hitched up to buggies for a spin in the meadow or down the road. Guests can try their hand at the increasingly popular sport of ski-juring! This is a sport where skiers are pulled behind a horse. Several mares are usually in foal to the Holsteiner stallion. Their foals can be seen cavorting around the paddocks from the sundeck.

Many guests bring their own horses and enjoy the miles of trails and training facilities at the farm.

OPEN:	Year round
GUEST ROOMS:	16 guest rooms, all rooms with private baths, phones and air conditioning.
RESTAURANT:	Breakfast, lunch and dinner served daily. Complimentary snacks. Lounge.
CREDIT CARDS:	Diners Club, MasterCard, Visa, Choice
RECREATION:	On premises: cross country skiing, jogging, pool, walking paths, picnic areas, indoor games, volleyball, ping pong, horseback riding. Nearby: Fishing, lake, tennis and antiquing.
RESTRICTIONS:	No pets in rooms.
EXTRAS:	Children under 16 free, meeting space, Dutch, German and French spoken, babysitting, handicapped facilities.
RATES:	$55-$65 per room. (Tax 6.5%)

DIRECTIONS:
Route I-66W to Front Royal. Take Exit 55 for 340Sthrough Luray, 6 miles south of Luray, turn left onto 624 then left onto 689, right onto 626. Inn is ¼ mile on right.

STANLEY VIRGINIA

LINDEN ROW

First & Franklin Streets, Richmond, Virginia 23219
(804) 783-7000

At Linden Row guests capture the essence of Richmond's historic past while enjoying the finest of the city's accommodations. The inn's location on stately Franklin Street makes it ideal for the business traveller and other visitors because of it's proximity to shopping, historic attractions, and to the downtown business district.

Linden Row was built during the 1840's and lovingly restored in 1988. The original seven townhouses are a Registered Historic Landmark. The 140-year-old Greek Revival architecture remains intact as do many of the original interior features such as marble mantles, pocket doors and chandeliers. The inn's guest rooms are furnished in part with authentic late Empire and early Victorian pieces.

While Linden Row preserves the past in many ways, it also offers the comforts of the present. All guest rooms have modern private baths, remote-control cable television, direct-dial telephones and individual heating and cooling systems. Each room has a worktable for business guests. Meeting rooms are available for up to 25 people, and there is valet as well as on-street parking.

Many of the inn's 16-foot-ceiling rooms overlook a brick-walled urban garden where light dining and refreshments are served on the patio in season. The dependencies of the original homes have been restored in the garden and offer guests Garden Quarters which have their own private entrances. No two Garden Quarters are alike, and all are available at rates that are even more attractive than those in the main part of the inn.

Guests also will find a blend of past and present in the dining room

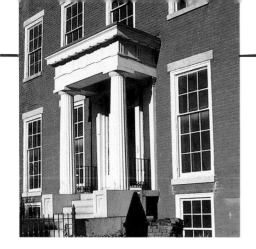

where breakfast, lunch and dinner menus feature American fine dining selections complemented by historic and period dishes. The same combination of selections is available for groups reserving the meeting room.

As a guest at Linden Row you will follow in the footsteps of famous residents and visitors. At one time a fashionable school for young Southern ladies, Miss Jennie Ellett's School (now St. Cather-ine's School), was located at No. 112 in Linden Row. Among its early alumnae were Irene and Nancy Langhorne. Irene was to become the famous Gibson Girl while Nancy was later known as Lady Astor, the first woman to sit in the British Parliament.

Undoubtedly the most famous name connected with Linden Row is that of Edgar Allan Poe, who lived across the street. In his poem, TO HELEN, Poe's "enchanted garden" is believed to have been inspired by the lovely gardens around which Linden Row was built. And it was here, as a resident at No. 110, that Mary Johnston wrote LEWIS RAND, following her best-seller of 1900, TO HAVE AND TO HOLD.

Linden Row, with its history and heritage, is "Richmond's Own." And its intimate atmosphere and gracious, unhurried service mark it as Richmond's only true "inn."

OPEN:	Year round
GUEST ROOMS:	73 guest rooms and suites, all with private baths, remote-control cable television, direct-dial telephones, work areas and individual heating and cooling systems.
RESTAURANT:	Breakfast, lunch and dinner served.
CREDIT CARDS:	American Express, Visa, MasterCard
RECREATION:	Nearby: museums, theatre, antiquing, shopping, historical sites.
RESTRICTIONS:	NONE
EXTRAS:	Meeting space, valet parking, handicapped facilities, dry cleaning.
RATES:	$70-$175 per room. Continental breakfast included. (Tax 9.5%)

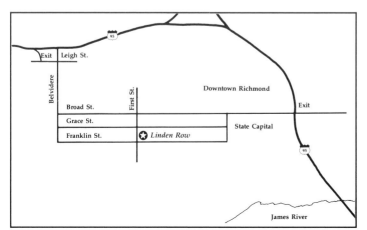

DIRECTIONS:
From North, I-95 or from West I-64: Take Exit 13 Belvidere Street off I-95/64. Follow US 1/301 South by turning left on Leigh, then immediately right on Belvidere. Go five blocks and turn left on Franklin. Linden Row is on left at First and Franklin.

RICHMOND VIRGINIA

MARTHA WASHINGTON INN

150 West Main Street, Abingdon, Virginia 24210

(703) 628-3161

Located in the far southwestern corner of Virginia on Daniel Boone's Wilderness Trail is Abingdon's own country inn. Elegant parlors, guest rooms individually furnished with classic antiques, delightful afternoon tea and delicious southern fare are only a sampling of the graceful refinement which characterizes the inn.

The main structure of the inn (now called the Mansion Wing) was built from 1830 to 1832 by General Francis Preston for his wife, Sara Buchanan Campbell Preston, who was the niece of Patrick Henry.

The home remained in the Preston family until 1858, when it was sold to the Hoston Methodist Conference to serve as Martha Washington College. The college immediately began construction of various wings to serve as dormitories and classrooms. Over the years the college continued to build additional facilities as necessary. During the Civil War the college even served as a hospital when the girls from this private finishing school cared for wounded Confederate and Union soldiers. The majority of ghost stories for which the inn is famous have their origins during the "War Between the States".

Due to declining enrollment and impact of The Great Depression, the college was forced to close in 1931. The building remained idle until 1935, when it was opened as the Martha Washing-

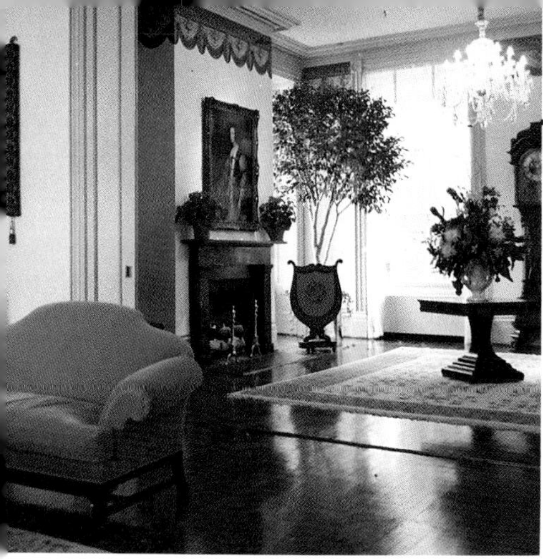

ton Inn. The inn changed hands several times before it was purchased by The United Company in April, 1984. Some $8.5 million was then spent to completely restore the inn to it's original resplendent ambience.

Without question, the features, the facilities and the furnishings which the inn offers are exquisite. There is a private social club, a white linen restaurant featuring the finest in Continental and regional cuisine, and two lounges.

There are numerous activities in the area which guests may enjoy. In addition to the Candlelight Tour of Homes each Christmas, the Burley Tobacco Festival in the fall and the Virginia Highlands Festival in the summer, Abingdon has many fine antique shops and a multitude of interesting art and craft shops from which to choose. Across the street is the world famous Barter Theatre. The Virginia Creeper trail, a hiker's delight, covers nearly four miles of beautiful Virginia countryside and begins only one mile from the inn. If you prefer, continue your journey along the scenic splendor of the Blue Ridge Parkway.

Whatever you choose to do, visit the Martha Washington Inn in Abingdon, Virginia where folk art, collectibles, antiques,mountain crafts, hiking, biking, plus a host of other activities await you.

OPEN: Year round

GUEST ROOMS: 61 guest rooms and suites, all with private baths, phones, TVs and radios. Some with jacuzzis, steam showers, and fireplaces.

RESTAURANT: Two restaurants. Breakfast, lunch and dinner served daily. Lounge available. Closed Christmas Eve at 2:00 pm until 2:00 pm Christmas Day.

CREDIT CARDS: American Express, Diners Club, MasterCard, Visa

RECREATION: On premises: jogging, library. Nearby: bicycles, fishing, golf, walking paths, picnic areas, sauna, theatre, outdoor pool, lake, tennis, and antiquing.

RESTRICTIONS: No pets

EXTRAS: Elevator, meeting space, handicapped facilities. Interpreter of European languages

RATES: $75-$360 per room. (Tax 7%)

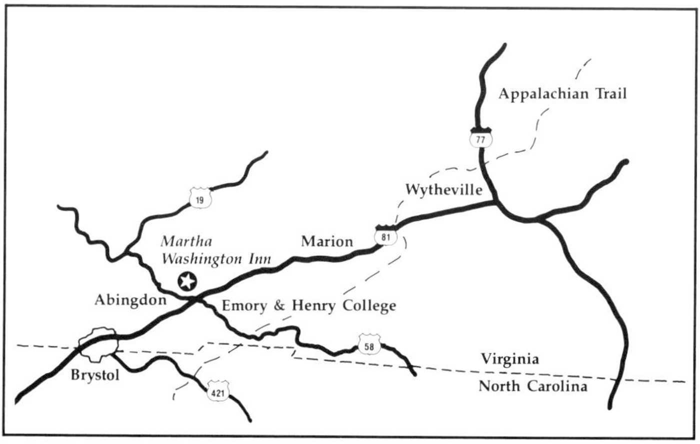

DIRECTIONS:
Two hours south of Roanoke, Exit 8 off of Interstate 81.

ABINGDON VIRGINIA

TRILLIUM HOUSE

Wintergreen Drive, Nellysford, Virginia 22958

(804) 325-9126

The Trillium House is a country inn on a country road at the entrance to Wintergreen, a popular year-round mountain resort. Built almost entirely of cedar, the inn offers rustic charm with modern amenities.

Guest rooms vary in size and are decorated with heirlooms which the innkeepers, Ed and Bettie Dinwiddie brought from their previous homes.

The Great Room with its 22 foot Cathedral ceiling and Jefferson sunburst window makes an imposing impression as guests enter the inn. A massive chimney and woodburning stove dominate this room.

The library with its extensive collection of reading material, or the recreation room with it's wide screen TV and VCR offer guests both quiet and social opportunities.

Dinner is homestyle with a single entre and served upon reservation in the inn's cozy dining room. Homecooked from her personal recipe box, guests enjoy Bettie's choice of fresh fish, poultry or beef. Her famous desserts bring back guests time after time.

The numerous sports activities of Wintergreen Resort are available to Trillium House guests. These include both cross-country and downhill skiing, swimming, fishing, sailing, hiking and more.

The clean mountain air is invigorating and the views of the Shenandoah Valley and Blue Ridge Mountains are breathtaking. Trillium House is the perfect spot to unwind and relax.

OPEN:	Year round
GUEST ROOMS:	12 guest rooms and suites, all with private baths. TV and phones available upon request in some rooms.
RESTAURANT:	Full breakfast served. Lunch is served by special arrangements. Dinner is served on Friday and Saturday and selected other nights by reservation.
CREDIT CARDS:	MasterCard, Visa
RECREATION:	On premises: golf, downhill and cross-country skiing, indoor pool and tennis. Nearby: boating, fishing and more skiing.
RESTRICTIONS:	No pets
EXTRAS:	Handicapped facilities
RATES:	$65-$140 per room. Includes full breakfast. (Tax 4.5%)

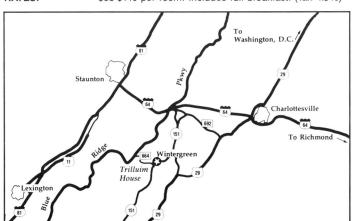

DIRECTIONS:
US 29 and I 64 to Exit 20 at Crozet. Go west on US 250 five miles, then turn left onto State Route 151. Continue on 151 for fourteen miles to State Route 664 and go four and a half miles to the Wintergreen gate. Ask the gate guard for directions to Trillium House.

WINTERGREEN VIRGINIA

TWO HUNDRED SOUTH STREET INN

200 South Street, Charlottesville, Virginia 22901
(804) 979-0200

Two Hundred South Street Inn is located in the downtown historic area of Charlottesville, Virginia, in the heart of the Blue Ridge Mountain wine and horse country. Every season offers an incredible choice of events - steeple chasing and world class jumping, wine festivals, Historic Garden Week, summer music festivals as well as the beauty of the surrounding Albemarle County.

Downtown Charlottesville is a small historic area with restaurants, shops, and entertainment. It is central to historic landmarks such as Jefferson's Monticello and his University of Virginia, Monroe's Ash Lawn, and Madison's Montpelier.

The inn is actually comprised of two residences, one of which was the home of the Wertenbaker family. Wertenbaker was Jefferson's friend, partner, and first Librarian at the University. Both buildings were completely restored in 1986, including the grand neo-classical veranda on the Wertenbaker house.

Inside, every bedroom is uniquely decorated with flowered Chintz, Oriental rugs, and 18th and 19th century English and Belgian antiques. The inn resembles some of the finest inns of Savannah and Charleston. Canopy beds, fireplaces, whirlpool bathtubs, and private sitting rooms are some of the options available.

A complimentary breakfast in either the guest rooms, the pleasant library or on the veranda is served on handsome black lacquer trays set with Ginori china and a vase of primrose. It may include fresh fruit, apple or cheese tarts, banana nut bread, brioche, jam, coffee or tea. Tea, Virginia wine and Jefferson Cider are served in the afternoon.

OPEN:	Year round
GUEST ROOMS:	20 guest rooms and suites, all with private baths, phones and radios. TV available upon request. Some have fireplaces, whirlpool baths and canopy beds.
RESTAURANT:	Continental breakfast served. Afternoon tea and wine complimentary. Restaurants adjacent to inn.
CREDIT CARDS:	American Express, MasterCard, Visa
RECREATION:	Nearby: Tennis, bicycles, antique shops, art museums, theatre, golf and historical sights.
RESTRICTIONS:	No pets
EXTRAS:	Babysitting, meeting space
RATES:	$80-$150 per room. Complimentary breakfast served. (Tax 8.5%)

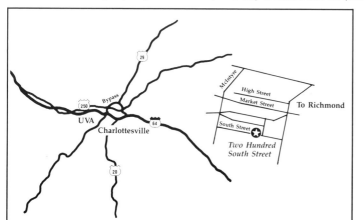

DIRECTIONS:
I-66 and US29 South: Take US29 to Route 250 Bypass East to McIntire Road exit. At second full traffic light, turn left onto South Street. The inn has a big wrap-around veranda. NOTE: There are one way streets in historic area.

CHARLOTTESVILLE
VIRGINIA

WASHINGTON HOUSE INN

W62 N573 Washington Avenue, Cedarburg, Wisconsin 53012
(414) 375-3550

The Washington House Inn was Cedarburg's first inn built in 1846. In 1886 the original structure was replaced by the present Victorian Cream City Brick building. The Washington House was used as a hotel until the 1920's when it was converted to offices and apartments. In 1983 its ownership changed hands and renovation began to restore the Washington House Inn to its original use. In 1986 the inn was listed on the National Register of Historic Places as part of the Washington Avenue Historic District.

The style of the inn is country Victorian and features an extensive collection of antique Victorian furniture, marble trimmed fireplace and fresh flowers everywhere.

The guest rooms are tastefully appointed with antiques, cozy down quilts, whirlpool baths, fresh flowers and other special touches.

The Washington House Inn serves an extensive continental breakfast with freshly prepared muffins, breads and cakes, fresh orange juice and delicious coffees. All of the bread and muffin recipes are from the Historic Cedarburg Cookbook.

Each afternoon, guests relax in front of the fireplace and socialize over white wine from a local winery and cheese from a local farm.

The entire town of Cedarburg is listed as a National Historic District with its many restored buildings. Walking tours are available daily.

Washington House Inn is only 30 minutes from Milwaukee. Guests may want to take in the cultural and sporting events offered by this great midwestern city including world class baseball and basketball.

OPEN:	Year round
GUEST ROOMS:	24 rooms and suites, all with private baths with whirlpools, TV with HBO, clock radio, pull out desks and telephones. Some with fireplaces.
RESTAURANT:	Breakfast is the only meal served. Several good restaurants are within short walk.
CREDIT CARDS:	American Express, Carte Blanche, Diners Club, Visa, MasterCard, Discover
RECREATION:	On premises: sauna. Nearby: antiquing, shopping, Historic Walking tour, winery tours.
RESTRICTIONS:	NONE
EXTRAS:	One day dry cleaning, iron and ironing board available, elevator.
RATES:	$49-$99 double occupancy. Includes continental breakfast. (Tax 5%)

DIRECTIONS:
Take I-43 to Cedarburg
Exit 17 (Washington
Avenue).

**CEDARBURG
WISCONSIN**

KIELY HOUSE HERITAGE INN

209 Queen Street, P.O. Box 1642
Niagara-on-the-Lake, Ontario, Canada L0S 1J0
(416) 468-4588

The Kiely House Heritage Inn speaks for the grace and elegance of an era past. Situated in Niagara-on-the-Lake, Ontario, Canada, the Kiely House Heritage Inn is truly a testament to the grandeur of the 19th century. Architecturally well-preserved and refurbished, its charming character is as captivating in the spring and summer as it is in the tranquil setting of the winter months.

A town saturated with cultural attractions and rich in historical resources, Niagara-on-the-Lake provides the perfect setting for the internationally acclaimed Shaw Festival Theatre. Open from May to October and December through February, the "Shaw" runs six

live performances each day featuring the works of George Bernard Shaw and his contemporaries.

Four local wineries host tours and tastings of Niagara wines. For the outdoor enthusiast, Niagara-on-the-Lake offers many hiking trails and parks to explore. Whether on foot, bicycle or cross country skis, Niagara-on-the-Lake is a town to truly appreciate for its beauty and allure.

One of Canada's oldest towns, Niagara-on-the-Lake was originally an Indian settlement known as Onghiara (this old Niagara) and was later the first capital of Upper Canada. Settled by English officers and their families, they built their homes on the scenic banks of

the Niagara River. In 1832 a wealthy Toronto lawyer built a stately summer home on land originally owned by Sir David William Smith, Surveyor General of Upper Canada. The home he constructed was of hand-hewn white oak beams, elegant and spacious. Set on an acre of land, the house had room enough for a large family, their servants and any number of friends for weekend parties. In 1900, a new wing was added with a two-story gallery. During its more than a century and half, the house has been a private residence for several fa-milies and was once pressed into service as officers quarters.

The parlours boast twin carved walnut fireplaces, original gilt-edged mirrors and magnificent crystal chandeliers. The parlours and the dining room are also showcases for the works of local artists.

Each of the twelve rooms is decorated in period style. Among the most popular is the former master bedroom, with its four poster canopy bed, fireplace, massive cherrywood wardrobe and doors leading to its private veranda overlooking the lush gardens.

A delicious a la carte breakfast and afternoon tea are served in the stylish dining room. The Kiely House Heritage Inn also packs picnic lunches and provides bicycles for guests to enjoy during their stay. For those who wish to maximize their relaxation, board games and a collection of classics are supplied to curl up with in front of the fire.

OPEN:	Year round
GUEST ROOMS:	12 guest rooms and suites, all with private baths and phones.
RESTAURANT:	Breakfast, lunch and afternoon tea only. Many fine restaurants nearby for dinner.
CREDIT CARDS:	American Express, MasterCard, Visa
RECREATION:	On premises: bicycling, cross country skiing, picnic areas. Nearby: tennis, antique shops, art museum, historic sights, theatre.
RESTRICTIONS:	No children under 12, no handicapped facilities.
EXTRAS:	Bottle of wine upon arrival, babysitting, meeting space
RATES:	$60-$125 per room. (Tax 5%)

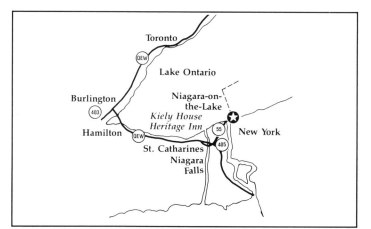

DIRECTIONS:
Queen Elizabeth Highway to Highway 58 North only. Surrounded by water on three sides.

**NIAGARA-ON-THE-LAKE
ONTARIO**

A FEW FINAL THOUGHTS

We have made great efforts to be sure the information about each inn is accurate. And, we are confident that it was at the time we put the Guidebook together. However, inns and innkeepers change, so we recommend you call and confirm important details before your visit to any of the Great Inns of America.

This guidebook would not have been possible without the help of the innkeepers who own and manage the Great Inns of America. Their personalities, charm, and humor are as varied as the inns they care for. Yet, with their dedication we are able to bring this book to inn lovers throughout the nation.

I also must give thanks to Cynthia Wein, our Membership Director. Cynthia searches for inns of quality to join Great Inns of America, and administers the programs we offer.

And, to our editors, who labored over copy, layout, and finances. Ray Dunn and Bill Klimkiewicz have read this guidebook a dozen times, looking for proper grammar, accuracy, and typos. Alicia Hitcho typed the book and spent many hours making sure the information on every inn was correct. Chris Larson, and his staff, drew the maps, selected the pictures and put the book together.

We also had help from the Great Inns of America staff, Nick Tensen, Gail Potts, and Leora Harrison. And finally, we are all grateful to Irv Davis whose steady hand and leadership assured this guidebook's success.

Bill Gilbert

GREAT INNS *of* AMERICA®

PHOTO CREDITS

1842 Bard Wrisley©
The Herbert Sheila Panori©
Yankee Clipper Inn Fredrik D. Bodin©
Lowell Inn Warren Reynold & Assoc.©
Gregory House Mark Merrett Studio©
Inn at Thorn Hill Ricke/Hults©

Cameron Estate Inn Cathy Barnett Charles©
The Point Geoffrey C. Clifford©
200 South Street Muncy & Muncy Photography©
Inn at Weathersford Courtesy of Country Inns Magazine©